CW01023268

Gende

First published November 2021

Printed by Panda Press (UK)
Contact details:
1 Newcastle Street,
Stone,
Staffordshire
ST15 8JU
England

Distributed and sold by Holy Cross Catholic Bookshop,
London, England
www.holycrossbooks.co.uk

Available from all good bookshops and online providers

All scriptural references are taken from
The CTS New Catholic Bible. (2008) 1st Edition.
London: Harper Collins Publications

ISBN 978-1-7398407-0-9

Foreword

Reading this fine work of Dr Charles O'Donnell, Gender Justice, a worthy successor to his earlier Sexual Justice, has been more than a pleasure. It has been an education and an opportunity to listen to the calm clear voice of faith and reason speaking to an ever- sensitive domain that has fallen victim in recent times to a mysterious level of confusion. There is nothing rabid or unreasonable here and no desire to insult. There is the courage of a believer. There is the wise compassion of a Christian doctor. And the result is an enriching, well-grounded insight into that astonishing action of the divine genius: "male and female he created them."

Naturally, one fears that this voice will not be heeded as it deserves but dismissed unheard. Surely, though, those who have ears will hear and benefit. But if that social dialogue in the search of truth which Pope Francis calls for in our post-Covid world is to happen, this work has a key contribution to make. May the seed, which this book is, be widely sown!

+Hugh Gilbert OSB
Bishop of Aberdeen
September 2021

Contents

Statement of Intent

Message to those persons who self-identify with a gender different from that which was assigned to them at birth based upon their sexual organs.

Gender Justice is not a judgement about your honesty. Your sincere spontaneous feelings are not sinful. You deserve to be respected and cherished. You are a child of a God who loves you with an infinite love.

Catholics believe in *Gender Justice!* Justice is the application of truth to protect wellbeing.

Gender Justice offers a Catholic perspective on why you experience these feelings and if you find them distressing and proposes ways to help you gain internal peace and happiness.

Gender Justice is a genuine approach to offer you and those around you justice where the sensible balance of rights and responsibilities is the guiding principle.

Introduction

The Catholic Church sees "sexuality *(i.e. Church language for gender)* as a fundamental *(i.e. Church language for innate)* component of one's personhood. (1) Catholics believe a person is made either male or female; gender is a binary (twofold) distinction. It is not an acquired attribute of personhood; it is to use the English saying "in the bones." This belief is defended by the Church both from reason (2) and from divine revelation in the Bible. (3)

This book explains why Christian anthropology suggests that it is an act of great injustice both to the individuals concerned and to the wider society to propose that gender is something that is primarily acquired from life experience or that gender exists in more forms than male or female. It also explains why the gender of a person is informed by their sexual characteristics and reproductive capabilities. Sex and gender for Catholics are two sides of the same coin.

The Christian vison is that gender is an essential innate difference between two equal modes of being human: male and female. It is like species or the composite material–spiritual (soul) make up of human beings; they are innate. Gender is not primarily decided or formed by perception or choice. Anybody who cannot believe this concept of gender is mistaken in their belief. They need to be loved and cherished but not told it is a normal human variant.

Clearly, the correct perception of gender, like any reality in the world, can be adversely influenced by things like false education or detrimental psychological and physical processes. This is a process of damage to a design not a prima facie occurrence.

An alternative secular view is that gender is primarily an acquired perception gained by the psychological process called conditioning or rehearsal. There are numerous different theories of how this can occur. (4)

At first sight, the protagonists of the new ideas about gender seem to say some very reasonable things! But the wording requires deciphering. Judith Butler, a leading philosopher cited in new ideas about gender, said: "I do know that some people believe that I see gender as a 'choice' rather than as an essential and firmly fixed sense of self. My view is actually not that. No matter whether one feels one's gendered and sexed reality to be firmly fixed or less so, every person should have the right to determine the legal and linguistic terms of their embodied lives". (5)

The "legal and linguistic terms of their embodied lives" is where the debate starts. This means the person can decide, irrespective of any biological reality, their gender. Gender identity has implications for society concerning the purpose of human existence. It matters what the terms man and woman mean. Or are they just humans with no more difference than a few pieces of anatomy? It matters whether sexual attraction to and activity with should involve a person of the opposite gender or whether it is irrelevant. And most of all, it matters whether children are optimally nurtured by a female mother and male father or whether any gender care partnership or solitary parent suffices.

Thus, gender is a question of justice. This book is about gender justice.

The gender debate has sadly become one where labels such as discriminatory are ascribed to the position of those who cannot accept the new ideas about gender. The Church abhors discrimination which is an unjust restriction of rights. The Church holds its beliefs because of a sincere reasoned argument supporting legitimate restriction not discrimination. For example, it is clearly racial discrimination if a public toilet sign says white people only. But it is not sexist discrimination to display a sign saying women only. This is a legitimate restriction.

In any dialogue it is important that those who hold opposite views ask why this is so. Also, as a minimum the opponents should extend the courtesy of respecting free speech and not stifle this by pejorative judgements about the malice of others. This book subscribes to these guiding principles.

Chapter 1

What Are the Differences Between Traditional Beliefs About Gender Versus Gender Ideology?

There are two conflicting definitions of what gender is:

• Gender is being either masculine or feminine which corresponds to different ways the male or female person communicate, have feelings and form relationships. It is innate. It corresponds with male or female sex. It is like a living animal is a human being or non-human being; there is no spectrum. It is a given binary (two-options only) reality. It is informed by sexual characteristics and reproductive capabilities.

• Gender is the thought of what sex I perceive myself to be irrespective of biological sex. Consequently, there is a spectrum. It is a variable (multiple-option) reality. It is not necessarily informed by sexual characteristics and reproductive capabilities. Beliefs that gender is binary are considered false because they are just seen as the product of upbringing conforming to societal norms of what makes a boy or a girl rather than any overriding innate predisposition.

For Christians, gender is as innate as saying a living being is either a human being or a non-human being. There is no middle ground, no room for debate; it is a fixed essential (innate) reality. It is typically revealed by sexual characteristics and reproductive capabilities. But it is important to stress sexual characteristics are one common, frequently occurring result of masculinity and femininity but not the primary definition.

For many modern secular sociologists, gender is primarily the socially acquired perceptual difference between being feminine,

masculine or another newly conceived gender type. (6)
The new ideas may be placed under the umbrella term Gender Ideology and the old under the umbrella term Essentialism.

The new ideas about gender constitute both a theory and an ideology. A theory is a set of ideas that is intended to explain something. An ideology is a set of ideas, not necessarily evidenced based, held by a group of enthused followers, for reasons that are not purely epistemic and that seeks to effect change.

Gender Ideology

Arguably the most well-known Gender Theory supporting the Ideology is called Performatism. About 30 years ago, philosopher Judith Butler called upon society to create "gender trouble" by disrupting the binary view of what is gender. (7) She argued that binary gender, rather than being primarily an essential inherent quality pointed to from biological sex and reproductive capabilities, is simply two modes of behaviour which are conditioned by societal norms of what makes a boy or a girl. Thus, binary gender is an illusion, a false perception of what gender really is. Real gender in a being gifted with rational thought is what the individual perceives it to be for themselves.

Thus, Performatists say that that there are not necessarily any primary innate essential causes of gender that can be ascertained a *priori* (from deduction), a *posteriori* (from observation) or a *revelatione divina* (from divine revelation.) Gender is for Performatists what the person comes to believe is their gender.

The Performatist Theory has the following behavioural implications that are summarised in the acronym DRIPS.

D Descriptive

Gender is not necessarily **descriptive** of any purpose connected to reproduction and nurturing. The labels of male and female, masculine and feminine, are not labels that delineate purpose like being a car is a vehicle to travel from A to B. Rather, they are labels that have no intrinsic immutable meaning; the meaning is unique to the person who adopts them, like "I am a long-haired person", or "I am a blue-eyed person". For example, the Australia National University's Gender Institute Handbook suggests that "gestational parent" is preferable to "mother", while "non-birthing parent" should replace "father". (8) Similarly, breast feeding becomes chest feeding.

R Restrictive

Gender is not binary **restrictive.** This means that there are potentially an infinite number of genders as each person establishes their own by psychological processes. Often to give some sense to the classification, advocates normally pick a number. For example, a BBC sex education programme put the number around 100. (9) Understandably there are calls for those who identify with a gender discordant with their anatomical sex to have access to medical and surgical therapies to "correct" the purported misalignment.

I Instructive

Gender is not necessarily **instructive** (pointing to, educating) about a deeper difference between masculine and the feminine in terms of any inner predisposition about how they communicate, feel emotions or form relationships. For example, writing in The Second Sex (10), the philosopher Simone de Beauvoir famously wrote: "One is not born a woman but becomes one." This claim created space for the belief that one may be born as female in the biological sense, but the gender of woman is a product of navigating a series of social norms to figure out how to be a woman.

P Prescriptive and Proscriptive

Because masculinity and femininity are not fixed realities heterosexuality (masculine-feminine sexual attraction) is not **prescriptive.** This is because if real gender is an individual perception, it means for one person their concept of masculinity may lead them to heterosexual relations, for others it may not. Similarly, because the sex organs and reproductive capabilities do not inform about gender, these biological realities have no more prescriptive role of heteronormativity (humans are designed to be heterosexual) than say the hands; some see the hands as means to become plumbers, and others see the hands as means to become surgeons. New ideas about what defines gender mean that biological realities cannot be used to be **proscriptive** of homosexuality or male pregnancy. The prescriptive and proscriptive implications of the new theories were aptly summarised by Judith Butler in her book *Gender Trouble.* (11) Her purpose, as she says in the subtitle of the book, is the subversion of identity—to force readers to question the standard categories of "male" and "female"—with the idea that this subversive project is for her the fundamental goal of gender study.

S Spousal Relationships

Gender does not dictate or inform about **spousal relationships.** Marriage, for those who subscribe to the new Gender Ideology, is a sociological construct. It is an invention of mankind just like different forms of government monarchy, dictatorship or democracy. Marriage is not an essential calling from nature inscribed on human nature by God that optimises the lived expression of the intimate relationship between masculine and feminine persons. The Gender Ideologists should be commended for their honesty when it comes to marriage. Correctly, many propose that for example gay and lesbian "marriage", rather than being a path to liberation, is just a new binary restriction stating who is and who is not respectable; it just creates a new underclass like bisexuals or polysexuals who cannot marry. Judith Butler candidly noted that the task at hand should ultimately be to "rework and revise the social organisation of friendship, sexual contacts, and community to produce non-state-centred forms of support and alliance." (12) Consent, choice and tolerance alone determine what constitutes good sexual relations.

Gender Essentialism

Christian anthropology holds traditional views about gender. This is called Essentialism. Gender Essentialists do not deny the effects of perverse education, the environment (psychological factors) or biological (physical diseases, genes and hormone) factors shaping the way gender is perceived, but it is modifying an inherent design not primarily forming it.

For Essentialists, gender is like the deeper meaning to be found in a newly conceived being from human gametes. It is not just a living bunch of cells that acquires its species as time passes; it is a human species with inherent rights irrespective of activity.

Gender Essentialists believe that gender is a given essential component of what it means to be human in terms of how men and women communicate, express feelings and relate. A person is either male or female. It therefore leads to conclusions about fulfilling human behaviour that are descriptive, restrictive, instructive, prescriptive, proscriptive and spousal.

This means the spiritual, psychological, anatomical and physiological differences between men and women help to describe the purpose of a fulfilled human existence. They restrict the number of genders to two. Gender instructs (points to, educates) about the deeper difference between the masculine and the feminine. Similarly, biological realism dictates that heterosexuality is prescriptive and homosexual sex is proscribed. Likewise, female pregnancy and breast feeding are prescribed, and artificial male pregnancy and male breast feeding are proscribed.

This is the summary of the debate.

Chapter 2

Why Do People Believe Gender Ideology?

Nobody fully knows the mind of another! One can only speculate reasons. It would be very naive and insulting to suggest that the protagonists of these ideas do not say some sensible things. Errors only get perpetuated when there are elements of truth in the propositions.

Also, when an error is believed by an adversary, Christians are obliged to look deep into the heart of the person and love them. That involves many things, including looking for reasons why their culpability may be impaired, praying for them and never subjectively judging them.

A common thread to those who espouse Gender Ideology is the hurt that has been perpetuated by systems, often given tacit or overt support by Christian people, that greatly undermined the infinite value of women, persons who self-label as having a same-sex attraction and those who sincerely believe their gender is discordant with their anatomical sex. On a psychological level, Gender Ideology may in part be an acute dissociation from reality to defend the individual protagonist from a world that they found to be threatening especially from the time of early childhood.

Possibly four classical errors of interpreting reality led to the wrong conclusions about gender.

Two of the errors were made by Essentialists and two by Performatists. These errors were:

1. Inference-Observation Error

Inference-observation error involves seeing something and

then making an inference using a false logic.

For example, inference-observation confusion could involve seeing someone driving a fancy car, and believing that they observed someone who is rich, when in practice they merely inferred that that person is rich based on their car, rather than observed it.

This type of error occurred in interpreting the phenomena of intersex persons. Intersex persons constitute about 2% of the human population. It also occurred when interpreting anthropological studies of unique communities where a third gender was an accepted norm.

2. Root Cause Analysis Error

There is a lot of understandable pain, anger and resentment in the writings of the new Gender Ideologists that is explained by many historical and contemporary injustices that they have recognised, including the sins of Catholics.

A root cause is defined as a factor that is deemed to be the primary causation of a nonconformance with what is deemed to be correct practice and should be permanently eliminated through process improvement. The root cause is the core issue—the highest-level cause—that sets in motion the entire cause-and-effect reaction that ultimately leads to the problem(s).

For example, if a patient dies because of a surgical procedure, many factors may have contributed. These may include poor surgical training, faulty equipment, bad operating technique, overworked nurses or competing egos in the operating team distracting the surgeons from a primary focus on patient wellbeing. But when the investigative team look at the death, they work backwards and find the root cause of all these observations was a patently under-resourced hospital that served to put patients at risk before any of the other factors could come into play.

In the sphere of gender, the following true observations were made:

1. People with gender dysphoria were ridiculed. Gender dysphoria is an intense internal anguish experienced by a person who does not perceive their gender to be the one they were assigned when they were born.

2. People who self-identified with a non-heterosexual sexual orientation were persecuted.

3. People who did not conform to a stay-at-home wife and mother or out-to-work husband and father were censured.

4. Women who conceived children outside of marriage were ostracised.

5. The Judeo-Christian teaching which guided mainstream thought in Western society for centuries that men are the head in a marriage partnership was often interpreted in a domineering, misogynist and patriarchal manner. It was a very commonly observed distortion of the intended meaning, sacrificial leadership.

Root Cause Analysis applied to these real problems deviated from the true root cause (false moral reasoning) and made gender the causal issue to be corrected.

3. Abbreviated Essentialism Error (Reductionism Error)

This error is the practice of analysing and describing a complex phenomenon in terms of a simple constituent, and then this is said to provide a sufficient explanation. It is like the person who says the only problem that caused the 2008 financial crisis was the banks or the only problem causing global warming are coal-fired power stations. These statements clearly are not true as there is a catalogue of contributors.

Performatists were remarkably familiar with their opponents making false promulgation of what Essentialists mean by being masculine and feminine. It may have contributed to their rejection of Essentialism.

For example, it was not uncommon for protagonists of binary gender to say a man is defined as a man if he has a penis. The implication is that if the penis is cut off he is less than a man or that if he does not father children, especially a son, thus demonstrating his manhood, he is less than a man!

However, when Christianity speaks of inherent masculinity and femininity, it means they have their primary roots in metaphysical qualities (beyond measurement, things like love, truth, peace and joy). It is not possible to have two kilograms of masculine or ten inches of feminine. This is clearly absurd. The potentiality for gender is written into the soul and manifested in the body.

4. Exaggerated Essentialism Error (Hyperbolic Error)

This involved Essentialists adding a long list of non-essentials to the essential list of being a woman or a man.

The new Gender Ideologists observed a collection of indefensible assertions and then falsely concluded that there are no essentials. It is the case of "throwing out the baby with the bath water." This is missing the important thing when swamped by a lot of irrelevancies.

All boys wear blue, all girls wear pink is the paradigm that epitomises the ridiculousness. But the list was endless: boys play football, girls do not; boys like science, girls like arts; boys are doctors, girls are nurses; boys wear trousers, girls wear dresses; etc.

When gender is defined by an exaggerated script of actions to be carried out that makes a real woman or real man, understandably a rejection is elicited by those who appropriately see the list as absurd, or do not do it or like to do it "correctly".

Exaggerated Essentialists give credence to the false idea that good Catholic men father lots of children, good Catholic women get pregnant ten times. This may be true for some, but not for all.

For those that believe in Gender Ideology, all things have importance in the defining process of making gender, be it the colours assigned to children (blue for boys, pink for girls), the common length of hair (men—short, women—long), the toys children play with (boys—soldiers, girls—baby dolls), the jobs young people aspire to (girls—secretaries, boys—plumbers) and all of the other stereotypical behaviours and interests individuals are "supposed" to embrace. Superimposed on this are the more serious matters of motherhood, fatherhood, sexual attraction, marriage and the nurturing of children.

All of these things form a package which those who back the new ideology use as evidence to construe that throughout history, gender roles (which for them define gender) have been put in place based on social conventions (constructs) depending on if a person has a penis and scrotum or a vulva and a vagina.

There is some truth in these new ideas. If we look back at history, we can easily identify how certain gender expressions have shifted or even completely reversed. A short list of these includes high heels, makeup, wigs and the colour pink—all of which were originally or primarily associated with masculinity and the "male" gender, while now they are largely embraced by the "female" gender.

The origin of high heels, for example, can be traced back to the 16th century where soldiers wore them to help secure their feet in stirrups. High heels had found their place on the feet of not only the male soldiers, but also aristocrats and royals in many parts of the globe who wore them to look taller and more formidable, and to keep their robes out of the dirt on the roads.

Overall, Exaggerated Essentialism often gave a sense that authenticity as a male or female is in the individual's own hands being determined by whether or not a person performs all of their roles in a socially acceptable manner. Not surprisingly the Performatists concluded nothing is essential and that it is behaviour that determines gender.

In summary Gender Ideology is the erroneous misinterpretations of reality that possibly, in part, can sadly be accredited to historical misrepresentations of the Christian message.

Chapter 3

Intersex Persons and Gender

Advocates of Gender Ideology put a lot of weight on the existence of intersex persons as a proof of gender fluidity and therefore "scientifically" supporting the new ideology. (13) The idea is that since sex as defined by sex organs, chromosomes, genes, hormone profiles etc shows variability in the human population then this observation can be used to support the idea that gender is similarly a variable reality.

Intersex people are individuals born with any of several variations in sex characteristics including chromosomes, gonads, sex hormones or genitals that do not fit the typical definitions for male or female bodies. Though the range of atypical sex characteristics may be obvious from birth through the presence of physically ambiguous genitalia, in other instances, these atypical characteristics may go unnoticed, presenting as ambiguous internal reproductive organs or atypical chromosomes that may remain unknown to an individual all their life.

Fig. 1 Classification of sex differences

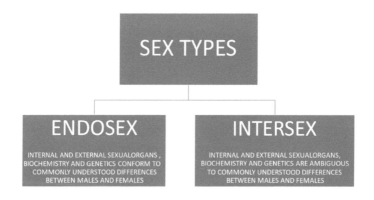

Estimates vary, but about 2% of the human population are intersex and 98% are endosex. (14) The variation between intersex and endosex individuals are usually very slight. For example, the person may have slight aberrations of the external genitalia. But the range of intersex conditions embraces differences that can be very substantial. There are a broad range of conditions and a huge amount of biological variability.

For those that need a simplified revision course in sexual differentiation, as the scientific knowledge currently stands, typically, it is for males to have 46 chromosomes, one of which is X and one of which is Y. Males have a gene on their Y chromosome called SrY (Sex related Y Chromosome Gene that codes for male development). Males have relatively high levels of the hormone testosterone and develop a penis and testes. Females typically have 46 chromosomes with two X chromosomes. Females do not have a SrY gene. They have relatively high levels of oestrogen hormone and develop a vagina and ovaries.

Individuals who believe in Gender Ideology have their beliefs strengthened when opponents say something like all people with XY chromosomes are males; this is not true in the literal sense. There are lots of people walking around with XY chromosomes who have the anatomy of female supermodels, behave like women, identify themselves as a woman and would be recognised as a woman by the Church.

But it is not a fair judgement because when the statement is made XY = male, it presupposes that XY means non-corrupted XY. It is like saying a person with a million pounds is always a wealthy person; the statement is true because it presupposes that the million pounds is real and not virtual and is accessible not subject to legal spending restrictions. The Church has thus correctly taught, given the assumed reasonable preamble, when she says: "From the point of view of genetics, male cells which contain XY chromosomes differ, from the very moment of conception, from female cells with their XX chromosomes". (15)

Nevertheless, atypical findings need a coherent explanation if traditional beliefs about gender are true.

Fig. 2 cites a few of the more extreme intersex conditions.

Fig. 2 Examples of extreme intersex conditions

TYPICAL FINDING IN MALE AND FEMALE BODIES	ATYPICAL FINDING WHERE THE PERSON HAPPILY CONFORMS TO THE OPPOSITE GENDER (IN SCIENTIFIC SPEAK HAS A GENDER NON-CONGRUENT PHENOTYPE)
Males have 46 XY chromosomes	Swyer syndrome, 46 XY SRY gene absent, and these people look and behave like females
Females have 46 XX chromosomes and no SRY gene	De la Chapelle syndrome, 46 XX, SRY gene positive, and these people look and behave like males
Males have testes	CAIS (Complete Androgen Insensitivity Syndrome) 33 (Testicular Feminisation Syndrome), 46 XY, have testes, and these people look and behave like females
Females have high oestrogen levels	CEIS (Complete Estrogen Insensitivity Syndrome), 46 XX, have high oestrogen levels, and these people look and behave like males

Intersex conditions are not proofs of gender fluidity. If one sees a house and then the same house a day later with no roof the possible conclusion from these findings are:

Option 1. There is no fixed design, there is just a spectrum of variability of house design.

Option 2. There is a fixed design which has suffered some damage.

The same is true with human biology and the phenomena of intersex persons. The proofs that option 2 is the reality are as follows:

1. Firstly, any person who respects the scientific method is fully aware of the phenomena of widows. This means scientists are always ready to stand back and say there are many widows; things that were once thought by respected scientists to be true and later shown to be false. To think that in 2021 we have a full biological understanding of embryogenesis and our measurements of genes, hormones and anatomical structures has told us the full story is very naive. So using intersex persons with current understanding of biology as proof definitive of multiple genders is an act of scientific naivety.

2. If intersex phenomena were a proof of gender spectrum, the occurrence rate would on the balance of probability be distributed normally, i.e. there would not be 49% of the population who are clearly anatomically and physiologically male, and 49% of the population who are clearly anatomically and physiologically female.

3. If rare visible variations prove normality, then we are left using the same distorted logic with accepting absurdities about essentials of our human existence, for example:

• Ambras (or werewolf) syndrome (patients who have this disease are hairy all over, affected persons are said to look like a werewolf.) But we do not accept this as proof of species fluidity. We say the unfortunate individual has a rare disorder and needs to be treated. (16)

• Congenital phocomelia (born with no arms or legs.) We do not accept this as evidence of body image fluidity. Two arms are normal; no arms are an abnormality. (17)

• African albinism (white-skinned child from black-skinned mother and father.) We do not accept this as evidence of intra-familial racial fluidity. (18)

4. Believers in Gender Ideology are not racists. In fact, they have a proven pedigree of strong anti-racism. But using the intersex population as evidence for the belief in more than two genders is akin to the historical offensive use of structural differences in body shape such as skulls or bone length to alter our belief in species consistency. There are no second species, like there are no third genders. These are simply biological variations, just like blue or brown eyes or curly hair or straight hair; they have no ontological (inner being) meaning.

This comparison is valid because those that use intersex persons as proofs of gender fluidity say because there are clear differences in body structure in intersex persons this proves that gender is not simply male or female.

For Catholics, the fact that there are men and women and no third, fourth, fifth, etc. gender is as important as believing that irrespective of the colour of a person's skin or the shape of their face, bone structure or subtle genetic differences everybody is a human being of equal dignity not a second species, sub-species or inferior species.

These types of offensive racist beliefs have Charles Darwin as their most famous advocate. Darwin may have mitigation of culpability given the beliefs of some highly respected people in a colonial age that found it hard to reconcile the massive technological achievement differences between white and non-white races with species equality. Nevertheless, the writings of Charles Darwin leave no room for doubt that he saw African and aboriginal races of human beings as being inferior and quite different in the core of their being to those with less melanin (the chemical causing skin darkening) in their skin. (19)

Darwin referred to black Africans and aborigines as apes who look like men—anthropomorphous apes! It is something like ascribing the label of a sub-species. A sub-species is a category in biological classification that ranks below a species and designates a population of a particular geographic region slightly distinguishable from other such populations of the same species but still capable of interbreeding successfully.

Darwin wrote: "At some future period, not very distant as measured by centuries, the civilised races of man will almost certainly exterminate, and replace, the savage races throughout the world. At the same time the anthropomorphous apes as Professor Schaaffhausen has remarked, will no doubt be exterminated. The break between man and his nearest allies will then be wider, for it will intervene between man in a more civilised state, as we may hope, even than the Caucasian, and some ape as low as a baboon, instead of as now between the Negro or Australian Aborigine and the gorilla."

5. Similarly, with our increasing understanding of the human genome it shows there are varying amounts of primitive humanoid genes in all the different races. (20) Once again, this is not evidence of different species, inferiority of species or sub-species, but using the argument of intersex genetic variations being proofs of different gender, it becomes a disgusting tenable analogy.

The fact that black Africans seem to uniquely have some of the genes of the most primitive ancestor homo heidelbergensis found in the homo sapiens genome to date is similarly not proof that black people are a unique phenomenon. We are all just human with some variations in our genes in terms of species classification. Similarly, genetic variations in intersex persons do not justify making the leap to say these persons are neither male nor female.

6. If rare medical diagnoses are used as a means to define normality, then the practice of medicine becomes a nonsense. Medicine is practised assuming the belief that normality exists and if a variant from the norm is found it does not define a new type of humanity, it defines a damaged type of humanity, be it heart disease, fractured bones, schizophrenia or whatever.

When a baby is born intersex, it is important to wait and see how the child matures before making definitive decisions about gender assignment and corrective surgery. Decisions taken too early and without a full clinical work-up have led to great distress for many intersex persons. The decision is based upon the assimilation of scan findings, hormone levels, genetic studies and seeing how the child behaves. It is not a choice per se of the parents; rather, it is a considered judgement weighing up the factors listed. Usually, the correct choice is made and the individual grows up to be a contented, well-adjusted male or female. However, sometimes in good faith the decision taken was wrong. (21)

But errors of medical judgement are not proofs of gender fluidity. This is a proof of the limitations of medical science, a responsibility to conduct further research in sexual differentiation and a call to humility for clinicians lest they think they have all the answers in the year 2021!

7. Despite many biological variations, there are no new gametes (sperm and ova), there are no new means of

reproduction, there are no new gonads (testes and ovaries and there are no new genes or new chromosomes. New realities of being have their biological origins in different, new building blocks. Therefore, it is unreasonable to cite variations around the norm as evidence of new norms.

8. Finally, very occasionally in intersex conditions, it has been possible to raise the individual as male or female. They seem to be OK reared as either sex, for example in the recent past, some cases of the micropenis cohort. (22) These individuals are 46 XY SRY gene positive born with a micropenis and often small testes. Regarding choice of gender, male sex rearing resulted in satisfactory genito-sexual function and gender euphoria. But also, female gender raising also resulted in success; however, it required extensive feminising surgery and hormone treatments. They were offered this therapy in good faith because it was felt the penis would be non-functioning and only serve as a psychological trauma to the patient.

But there are lots of confounding factors to refute the idea that these cases are proof of gender fluidity.

The individuals who historically were raised as females had extensive surgery to construct female-type genitalia, removal of their testes and lifelong hormone supplements along with psychological conditioning. Most importantly, persons who are born with a micropenis usually have an identifiable inherited hormonal or genetic abnormality that can influence brain and body development of the unborn child. Thus, there were plenty of reasons to adulterate the innate gender other than a primary role of psychological conditioning. Of note, nowadays this cohort of patients are raised as males as the surgery required to fashion female genitalia is now considered disproportionate and these people are seen to be masculine.

Micropenis is usually caused by foetal testosterone deficiency which can be the result of a variety of conditions.

The most common is hypogonadotropic hypogonadism. Hypogonadotropic hypogonadism is a condition that occurs when the hypothalamus (the part of the brain that controls the autonomic nervous system and pituitary) does not secrete the hormones that stimulate the testicles to produce hormones (testosterone) necessary for normal maturation and reproductive function. Micropenis may also be found with genetic syndromes that can cause other malformations and learning disabilities. Or the condition may be idiopathic (have an unknown cause), so more investigative research is clearly required.

In summary, people who have an intersex condition deserve great sensitivity when being discussed, addressed or treated. They should not be used as pawns in a gender war! From reason, they are not evidence to support non-binary gender.

Chapter 4

Anthropology and Gender

Along with the use of intersex persons as "proofs" of the new ideas about gender, a variety of anthropological studies have been cited to give support to Gender Ideology. Anthropology is the study of humans in relation to distribution, origin, classification and relationship of races, physical character, social relations and culture.

For example, anthropologists who believe in Gender Ideology studied how Native American tribes viewed gender and sexuality particularly before European colonisation. (23)

"Two Spirited" was the name given by the Navajo tribe to people who identified as transgender. The Lakota people referred to transgender persons as Winkté, which refers to a person thought to be male at birth but then behaving as a female. Similarly, the Iroquois Cherokee tribal language included names for gender variations implying they were both acknowledged and respected.

But observation does not prove this is a good thing for human fulfilment; it just proves it happened.

A group of people may be observed to accept many types of identity or behaviours, but that does not prove these facets of human populations necessarily lead to human fulfilment. Many tribes worldwide have been found to be cannibalistic, engage in child sacrifice and expose their people to calls for ritual suicide. These are presumably not to be held as normative.

Also, when a small group of people are taken from a specific location, it cannot have any likely predictive value in the whole human population. This is because for samples to be predictive of the whole population, they need to be large, representative of all of humanity and be set against a properly constructed control group.

The Christian explanation for the damage we see all around us in the beauty of creation is that our good human nature suffered injury which is distributed in a variable way across time and geography. It is called original sin. So yes, gender discordance is found, but the positive acceptance, toleration or rejection of this as a fulfilling mode of being is highly variable. For example, Ancient Rome featured a myriad of, what could be understood, both then and now, experiences that transcended sex and gender norms. However, Roman society encouraged the marginalisation particularly of trans-feminine expressions, identities and non-binary sex assignments, seeing them as detrimental to human wellbeing. (24)

Across all cultures, all times and all locations, the overwhelming predominance of binary gender is clear. While it is true this does not scientifically prove that binary is the normal gender distinction for human beings, it is a powerful indication. Frequency of observation is not definitive of form unless it is 100%, but it is highly suggestive. When, for example, we observe that more than 99% of human beings have two legs when they are born, we conclude that it is normative for humans to be a bipedal being, and for those with one or three legs we call it an atypical variant of body form, not a new normal.

Finally, Otherkin are a group of people who identify as not entirely human. Otherkin believe their identity derives from things like reincarnation, ancestry or metaphor. (25)

Categories of Otherkin include Fictionkin, those who identify as fictional characters, Conceptkin, who identify as abstract concepts and Weatherkin, who identify as weather systems. Many are adamant this is not a religion. While there is an overlap with people who suffer mental illness, the subculture is populated by individuals who are highly intelligent, are not intent on forming a religion and have intact mental health.

The same type of anthropology that finds minority tribal identities and translates that into proof of normality would need to put Otherkins in the same pathway of "proof" for this being a true hybrid species (half-human, half-elf) hidden to most of us in the human population. It would be a hard sell in 2021 AD to convince most people this is a reflection of truth. Otherkin persons need to be loved and cherished but not reinforced in a mindset that is potentially very damaging for themselves and those they have responsibilities towards—just like those who identify as transgender.

Chapter 5

The Language of Gender

The idea known in linguistic circles as the Sapir–Whorf hypothesis is that language is the way an individual is taught to conceive the world. (26) As an absolute truth the idea has been basically discredited. But language does have some influence on thought especially for those who do not have the ability to critically analyse what they are being told. Children and young people who have not developed skills of critical appraisal are particularly prone to this. Many people believe that if the law or the teacher says x, then x must be true! Not so.

Advocates of Gender Ideology have made language a key target in their attempts to transform the way people think about gender and sex. (27) It was for the same reason that gay rights activists campaigned for gay marriage even when civil partnerships offered exactly the same rights and responsibilities. The activists knew language matters in terms of changing opinions.

In one way, Gender Ideologists have a point. Much of the gender-specific language that is used is both hurtful to those who suffer gender dysphoria and conveys ideas of activities that can only be done by men or women that are clearly absurd. Thus, it is perfectly reasonable to campaign, with a few sensible cautions in place, for these types of non-essential linguistic modifications. Fig. 3 offers some examples.

Fig. 3. Non-essential gender-modified language

ORIGINAL LANGUAGE	PROPOSED MODIFICATION
Mankind	Humanity
Chairman	Chairperson
Businessman	Representative
Policeman	Police Officer
Landlord	Owner
Manhole	Access-hole
Salesman	Salesperson
Fireman	Fire Fighter

It is similarly reasonable for a person to want to change their name from Paul to Sarah. Clearly, if a man wants to be known as Sarah, then so be it. Names do not have an inherent gender. In many countries where Spanish is the first language, Mary/ Maria is a common part of the name of boys and many Catholic priests adopt the name of Mary into their title in the English-speaking world.

But the battle over language goes further than these reasonable requests. It enters the realm of using language to subvert essential differences between men and women. This occurs by three techniques:

• The introduction of lexicons of gender types other than masculine and feminine (Fig. 4)

• Insisting that pronouns always be altered according to the desire of the person. For example, a person assigned male gender at birth who believes they are a woman requests to be addressed as she. Pronouns are words like he, she, his and hers.

• Suggesting titles become fluid in this way means that titles like husband, wife, mother, father, Mr and Mrs have their meaning changed to what the individual decides.

The Christian vison of what is best for people cannot unconditionally subscribe to these types of adulterations of language because they potentially subvert an essential component of the goodness of creation. If a person undermines the beauty of the work of an artist, they can de facto undermine the artist. It can be an offence against the first commandment. When asked which of all the laws of Scripture is the greatest, Jesus Christ responded with the command emphasising the supreme importance of our personal, respectful relationship with God: "You shall love the Lord your God with all your heart, with all your soul, and with all your mind". (28)

Christians believe the divine artist created a world with beauty inscribed in it. This truth was communicated in the account of creation in the Book of Genesis: "Male and female he created them" (29) and "he saw all that he made was good". (30)

Unequivocally affirming pronoun language changes is akin

to affirming that some people could be addressed as non-human beings, or perhaps an inferior race or that they could be thought of as beings without a soul (zombies) if they made a request. Language is the means human beings use to communicate their principles, and the goodness of male and female genders is a fundamental principle which underpins a host of essential rights and responsibilities concerning male–female relations, marriage and childcare.

However, pastorally, to ensure that persons who suffer gender dysphoria are addressed with sensitivity while at the same time avoiding insulting God, there are several simple options:

• The simplest is to use the chosen name, provided it is gender-neutral by being free from gender specific titles like Mr, Miss or Mrs.

• Using "their" or "theirs" maintains neutrality without imputing a false ontological change in the person.

• Theoretically, there is nothing objectively wrong in inventing new neutral pronouns. In some languages, almost everything is gendered, e.g. French; in others it is far less, e.g. English. So, for example, rather than addressing a person as she or he, it could become ze, and her and him could become hir. The problem with making new words is the confusion that results. If the new words are a charitable act to help suffering persons, then there is some merit. The problem is that the motive may be sinister, to use new words to communicate a false ideology rather than a compassionate method to alleviate the psychological distress experienced by people who suffer gender dysphoria.

This refusal to reverse pronouns can cause a false battleground. On one side is the argument of freedom of speech, on the other the freedom of the individual to self-identify and have that identity acknowledged. Both freedoms are not absolutes. Freedom of speech does not permit the racist, sexist or homophobic person to address others in crude language; the dignity of the person concerned is too great. Similarly, nobody should be permitted to make another person purposely offend a mark of dignity of another even if that person begs for it; for example, the man who wants to be called Fido because he feels himself to be a dog would correctly find that others would resist this address because it is perceived as an insult to his dignity. It would also be perceived as an insult to the dignity of his family.

The real battle is, what makes truth? Is truth given or self-made? In a pluralistic society where both views need to live side by side, the sensible middle-of-the-road compromises cited previously are usually the correct balance of rights and responsibilities.

For some transgender persons, the request for pronoun reversal is a cry of anguish; even the word "he" instead of "she" can cause immense psychological damage and risks the person doing self-harm to assuage the pain. For others, however, it is a trophy of assent, or it is a means to offend those who disagree with the new ideas of gender, and for some, it is just incidental on the level of "c'est la vie."

The assumption must always be the worst-case scenario to avoid traumatising a vulnerable person. Therefore, it is vital that other means of helping these suffering persons are put in place. Addressing the person by their chosen name provided it is gender-neutral and ensuring others are educated in the importance of this strategy is a balanced charitable response. Many bishops giving guidance to Catholic teachers who can be faced with this problem in the classroom have offered this type of sensible pastoral advice. (31)

Those asserting a transgender identity and/or seeking to "transition" often adopt new gender-defining names like Mr Smith becomes Miss Smith, and pronouns that reflect their desired identity and insist that others must use the chosen names and pronouns. Such use might seem innocuous and even appear to be an innocent way of signalling love and acceptance of a person. In reality, however, it presents a profound crisis: Catholics can never say something contrary to what we know to be true. To use names and pronouns that contradict the person's God-given identity is to speak falsely.

Catholics avoid using "gender-affirming" terms like Mr for Mrs or pronouns that convey approval of or reinforce the person's rejection of the truth because they love the person. There is no robust scientific evidence that such changes do anything to effectively console the person suffering gender dysphoria. It is not harsh or judgemental to decline to use such language.

In the broader culture, Catholics (and other Christians) are increasingly experiencing significant pressure to adopt culturally approved terminology. However, in no circumstances should anyone be compelled to use language contrary to the truth. The right to speak the truth is an inalienable right and should not be taken away by any human institution. Attempts by the state or employers to compel such language, particularly by threats of legal action or job loss, are unjust. A just society must love the truth, and truth must be accurately conveyed by our words. At the same time, clarity must always be at the service of charity, as part of a broader desire to move people towards the fulness of the truth

Finally, in a world of gender neutrality some strange things could occur. In such a world, there is no clear way to specify one's niece, nephew, aunt or uncle. If one refers to "my secondary biological parent's sibling's child," the identity of niece or nephew remains obscure. Similarly, is my "primary birthing parent's sibling" my aunt or my uncle? And is her "sibling" her brother or her sister?

If Holy Scripture changed, Genesis would state that God created "people" who could get together in different ways. Male, female, husband and wife, would be deleted. St Paul would address his readers with the salutation "Dear siblings."

Altering language without considering the unintended or intended side effects of the machination needs to be done with great caution. Ideologies come and go; they evolve into new forms very quickly, so regardless of beliefs, it is just wise to avoid big shifts in language to avoid standardising nonsense. When Neil Armstrong said "this is one small step for a man, one giant leap for mankind" everybody knows he was using mankind in the generic sense; nobody thinks he was making a discriminatory comment. Similarly, when people use manhole they do not think women cannot go down into the sewers if they so wish; women just normally have more sense and leave it to men! If language changes are made failing to see the many conflicting goods that can be damaged, the result may be a greater backlash and even more distress for those who suffer gender dysphoria.

Fig. 4 Examples of proposed new types of gender

GENDER TITLE	DEFINITION
Trans-woman gender	A person with male external genitalia feels they are a woman
Trans-man gender	A person with female external genitalia feels they are a man
Androgyne gender	The person feels they are part male and part female making a male–female hybrid
Bigender gender	The person feels they are both male and female at the same time
Agender gender	The person feels they do not have a gender; they are neuter
Fluid gender	The person feels that their gender varies over time
Queer gender	The person feels they have a gender that is outside conventional options
Multiple gender	The person feels they have many types of gender

Chapter 6

What Do Catholics Mean by Masculinity and Femininity?

Let us start by making it clear. Listening to some religiously minded people can lead to the conclusion that it is all about the genitals; it is not! Gender in the eyes of Catholic Christians is far deeper than this. One can be born without a penis, have an accident and lose a penis, or have an operation and have a penis amputated, and manhood is still present.

Also, sadly there is sometimes a bit of confusion in the way those who hold religious views explain the difference. The difference has been ascribed according to three incomplete explanations: stereotypical behaviours, polarised brain attributes or physical differences alone.

Stereotypical behaviours are expressed in ideas like women are nurses, men are doctors, women are cleaners, men are plumbers, boys play football, girls play netball, boys wear blue, girls wear pink. This is clearly nonsense.

Stereotypical behaviour theories are also expressed in historical family set-ups of homemaker mum and wage-earner dad. These similarly do not describe the difference. The mum-at-home, dad-at-work model had many reasons to exist beyond any intrinsic differences in males and females, including the breast feeding of infants before bottle feeds became available, short adult lifespans and the economic value of labour depended in the past mostly on physical strength (farm work, industrial labour, etc), and so the economic necessity for a family to survive was to send the most physically productive member of the marriage to be the wage earner, especially as wages were not far off subsistence.

Also, it is very dependent upon which country a person is born in. In rural Africa it is very common to see the women doing all the work in the fields and in the home! Nowadays, in the West, where the economic value of labour is much more related to intellectual pursuits, the wage earner versus homemaker role is much more fluid.

Similarly, the difference between men and women is not about polarised brain attributes. The idea that women alone are nurturing, intuitive and gentle, and men alone are assertive, innovative and mechanistic is not true. There are lots of assertive women and there are lots of nurturing men, etc.

But here is the difference. Women are made to be assertive, etc. in a feminine way, and men are made to nurture, etc. in a masculine way. We see it clearly when a man behaves like a woman or vice versa; it is a caricature and we can easily laugh if the person is doing this to amuse, and feel pity if that is how the person feels that they need to behave to be accepted by those around them.

Jesus Christ clearly confirmed the teaching in the Old Testament that human beings are either male or female. Christians listen to Jesus because they believe the evidence that he was God, and God does not make mistakes!

Christian anthropology proposes that gender is part of the innermost core of being. This is a crucially important point. Catholicism teaches that persons are not male and female just because of their biological sex (penis and vagina); persons usually have those sex organs because God has made them male or female. Anatomy is one of the ways that male or female identity is commonly revealed, but it can also be seen in so many other aspects of the body. Genetics, physiology, neurology and psychology all recognise the intrinsic differences between the sexes. These impact on the different ways that men and women communicate, experience the world, have feelings and form relationships.

Thus, Catholics understand gender to mean embracing a purpose, which is inscribed (blueprinted) into the soul and revealed through the body of a person. The only way that the workings of the soul can be identified is through the body; we cannot see our souls. Gender, masculinity or femininity, is a deep call to be a perfect man or a perfect woman by differences in the way men and women communicate, express feelings and form relationships. It is the work of a lifetime.

Responding to this call requires a body. In the most clear form, the body that can mother or father a child is a potent manifestation of the workings of the soul. Sexual love is another very clear pointer of the difference; the act of intercourse is obviously unique to male and female in anatomical, physiological (and spiritual) realms. But motherhood and fatherhood are also labels of spiritual attributes to be applied to all people the individual meets, single childless people are thus called to be (spiritual) fathers and mothers in the depths of their being.

Gender, male or female, is the sub-division in the blueprint in all human beings to be fully human. We see all manner of human behaviours (human expressions) including a considerable amount of debauchery around us. But to be a truly fulfilled human, as we are meant to be, is to seek virtue, to love our neighbour (and God!).

Even in day-to-day speech, we speak about those who display heroic virtues showing all that is best in humanity. They make us proud to be human; it is what human beings are meant to be. Conversely when we see the depths of depravity (rape, murder, child abuse, genocide, etc.) these are equated to a person being no better than a wild beast; it is perceived by most as something human beings are not meant to be. This type of inner calling of what it means to be human is expanded or sub-classified by what it means to be a masculine human or a feminine human.

According to the intention of the Creator, therefore, the manifestation of human nature in woman necessarily differs from its manifestation in man. These distinctions can be diminished or increased by education, imposition and custom but cannot be completely annulled.

It is important to note that these differences between men and women do not in any way imply inequality. The equality spoken about between men and women in the Bible is fundamentally a moral equality of the sexes. It is not about the size of the biceps or the hairs on the legs, which are usually very different! The moral law for man and woman, that is, the call and obligation to seek to do good and shun evil, are the same. To assume a lax morality is OK for the man (boys will be boys mentality) and a rigid one for the woman is an oppressive injustice and not equality even from the point of view of common sense. Likewise, woman's work, the way a person seeks to do good in the wider world, is therefore in itself of equal (equitable) value with that of a man, as the work performed by both is ennobled by the same human dignity. A stay-at-home mum is equal to a work-away dad and vice versa when performed virtuously.

The equality of masculine and feminine persons is thus an equitable not a mathematical manifestation of equality. For example, the female sex is in some respects inferior to the male sex! On the other hand, the female sex is in other ways superior to the male sex! But these inferiorities and superiorities are about mode of communicating not value.

For example, ascribing terms to females like the more beautiful and the weaker sex as statements of proven inferiority or superiority as measurable mathematical values are incorrect. The female sex is neither the more beautiful nor the weaker sex. The one designation is the invention of sensuality and of flattery; the other owes its currency to masculine arrogance. In an equitable way the female sex is as strong as the male, for example in endurance, patience, magnanimity and in quiet long-suffering, but it is not normally mathematically equal in terms of manual strength. Male form is just as beautiful as female form when seen as a comment about the whole person rather than a superficial glance at a male torso which often lacks the finesse of the female form.

There is a great deal of scientific literature documenting significant biological differences between the sexes. There is also a great deal of scientific evidence of the similarities between men and women. But rather than primarily engaging in a debate over biochemistry, anatomy and physiology, Christianity focuses the discussion on gender about what the differences and similarities mean for our understanding of how men and women are gifted to perform sometimes the same tasks and sometimes different tasks. This means while sexual intercourse, pregnancy and the nurturing of children are important pedagogies in the male–female dyad, there is much more to the subject.

Christianity proposes that men are men and women are women because of not what they can do, but how they are made to do it. It is like one can communicate to a friend by email or telephone; both get the message over, but they do it in different modes, and the results are both complementary (the message is reinforced by being received twice) and may be very different (one is given with more emotional understanding, and the other with more abbreviated precision; there is a place for both).

In day-to-day language, we often speak about the man revealing his feminine side and vice versa. For men it commonly means showing their emotions, for women being aggressive. The use of the words masculine and feminine in this way are not what the Church is talking about when it comes to masculinity and femininity.

To understand in a clear way what Catholics mean by femininity and masculinity (or in other words the call to act as father or mother, be it physically or spiritually), the works of St Edith Stein (32) and St Pope John Paul II (33) with their development of the concept of feminine and masculine genius (particular gifts) are a good place to start.

Edith Stein was a German-Jewish atheist philosopher who was recognised by her peers as being exceptionally talented. A brilliant writer and intellectual, she earned her doctorate in philosophy in 1916 and became a university professor, in an era when few women took part in higher education at all. She converted to the Catholic faith, became an enclosed nun dedicated to a life of prayer and was murdered in 1942 by the Nazis in Auschwitz because she was a Jew. She was recognised as a saint in 1998. St John Paul II was the visible leader of the Catholic Church on earth 1978–2005. A saint is someone believed to be very close to God in heaven.

They both recognised the universal belief that it is love (understood as self-giving and acceptance of another) that gives human beings their fulfilment, their purpose for existence. Human beings are made for love; in popular culture, "love is what makes the world go round". It counteracts the cold nihilism of the purpose of human life being a mere acquisition of material goods, money, sexual delights or a perpetuation of the race. Both also clearly recognised that love, just like truth, justice and joy, are spiritual not material qualities. Love cannot be measured. It is beyond the physical reality; it is metaphysical. It is impossible to have 10 inches or 2 kg of love.

This view of masculinity and femininity being primarily defined as unique ways of manifesting love as an essential to the purpose of being a male or female needs to be recognisable. Since we cannot see the soul gender can only be objectively recognised by the physical body "speaking" of the inner potentialities of the soul. Simply listening to expressed thoughts cannot carry the same objectivity standard because thoughts can change from minute to minute. The actions and structure of the body are the fixed window to the spiritual reality that is part of human existence being a man or a woman.

For men and women, there are "geniuses," or sensibilities, particular modes of loving (self-gift) inscribed on the soul and portrayed by the body that define masculinity-love and femininity-love. The person's masculinity and femininity are defined by the unique way he or she can give of him or herself, how they are made to love, in the home and workplace, private and public spheres and in the intimacy of the sexual embrace.

Putting one word to explain these geniuses, special gifts or sensibilities is difficult because one is trying to describe a metaphysical reality (unmeasurable) with physical (measurable) words. It is like trying to put into words the feeling of falling in love. Everybody agrees that falling in love exists, but no words can truly explain it because it is metaphysical reality. The same problem is true about describing God; no words can completely explain the nature of a spiritual reality.

A possible dyad (albeit with the provisos in place) requires the invention of a new noun, "sacrificity". To be perfectly masculine, to be the man one is made to be, to love as a man should love, is to have "sacrificity" of soul; the inner aim of man is to sacrifice himself for the good of others. To be feminine, to love as a woman should love, is to have "receptivity" of soul; the inner aim of woman is to be gifted with a special ability to be receptive to the needs of those around her.

Let's explore these terms and the evidence for the reality of these essential differences between men and women.

Masculinity

To be a man is a deep inner calling, an ontological voice to sacrifice self. This is how men are called to love. It is a call that is made by many women to men. Although many feminists do not realise it, they are calling for the perfect man, what it means to be the man they are made to be to come out and to disregard counterfeits. The numerous articles denouncing male domestic violence and calling upon other men to rise up to the challenge to defend women are an example of this. (34) The proof of the call is that the two antitheses of this sacrificity of being are an anathema to women.

The two extremes opposing "sacrificity of soul" are machismo and effeminacy.

EXTREME MASCULINITY	PERFECT MASCULINITY	INADEQUATE MASCULINITY
Machismo	Sacrificity	Effeminacy

There is an urgent need to temper the idea that a man is a man by exerting aggressive power. The phenomenon is called toxic masculinity or machismo. It leads to thinking being a real man is about exerting aggressive power, be it physical or mental, over others. Not surprisingly, this can result in serious harm to women by violence, sexual prowess, female suppression in the workplace and home or manipulative abuse. It leads to patriarchy and misogynism.

This urgency is highlighted by the understandable incredulity expressed by many women about men. It would be foolish not to recognise this in this age where at least 1 in 3 first marriages dissolve, 20% of children are left unintentionally with single unmarried mothers who are often not given material support by the father, and pregnant women are left by their boyfriends so that many feel abortion is their only choice. The conclusion is that there is no grand design for manhood in the hearts of men. The notion that masculinity is just a variable construct of society can then sound a likely explanation.

Equally damaging to women (and indeed to everyone) is the acceptance of effeminacy as a mode of expression of masculinity. Historically, the word effeminacy was used to describe a cohort of men especially in ancient Rome who were prepared to surrender themselves or forced to surrender themselves to other men for sexual gratification as a passive partner in a homosexual intimate relationship. They were despised for this. (35) It is just one rare manifestation of effeminacy. But this is not the full theological meaning of the word.

The theological meaning of effeminacy is a reluctance in a man to suffer for the good of others due to an attachment to pleasure. (36) It must be stressed that effeminacy as a vice is not the same thing as perfect femininity as a perfection given by God to women. Femininity is good, whereas effeminacy is disordered. In common day-to-day use of language, the words feminine and effeminate are often used interchangeably.

Effeminacy is especially abhorrent because it is much more common than machismo, and it is even accepted as OK. The passivity is framed as gentleness or a connectivity with feelings, the feminine side of a man or, worse still, the "gay" side of a man! Or it is framed as an honourable avoidance of interference in the affairs of others, a man who respects privacy.

This is not true; for a start, it is an insult to people who are women or people who express a same-sex attraction. To be gentle in the Christian sense of the word is to be calm, serene and moderate in actions even when adversity strikes. It is not to be a coward or just let things go or be full of superficial mannerisms like "touchy-feely!" The effeminate does not really care when others are being hurt; they just let it go.

Men are made to be sacrificial in their mode of being, in their way of loving, so as justice can flourish in society. Men are made to be sacrificial so as to refuse to use their power to evade service. It is not manly to use the material and physical advantages that men often acquire to simply drink and make merry. Men are men when they love to the point of sacrifice.

Men are made to be active not passive masculine, to be the type of general who leads from the front, taking the risks, not a general who sits 10 miles away from the battle with callous disregard for the wellbeing of the soldiers he orders over the top into battle. Sacrificity of soul is also demonstrated by the husband who heads a family by sacrifice of self, not the effeminate way of sacrifice of his wife and children for his own satisfaction.

A good example of the masculinity is man being given the gift to be the head of the family. This gift is meant to be used to sacrifice self, not a commandment to dominate. As such, it is both a joy and a burden of responsibility. In any relationship of equals, democracy cannot be the modus operandi for decision making else difficult decisions where no consensus has been achieved can get taken.

Having a person who freely promises to sacrifice self for the good of the other, and who finds his own inner fulfilment in this activity, is the key to the dilemma. Historically, the wedding vows included obedience. Sadly, all too frequently this was used as a means to subjugate women, but its true meaning was for a woman to place herself in "sub-mission" to another who is duty bound to sacrifice self. It was to be the subordinated (sub) to the mission of a man to sacrifice himself to the point of death (hence sub-mission/obedience). It was using human words to communicate a divinely instituted insurance policy of immense value to the dignity of women and the proper functioning of marriage. It is all about service not power!

Men as they are made to be are people like fathers who, despite their faults and failings, get up in the morning, go to do a job they find unpleasant, come home with a smile on their face, use their wages to feed the family, do not expect dinner on the table and most certainly are never violent. Similarly, the man who stays at home caring for his children while his wife works outside of the home, despite perhaps longing for another occupation and still maintaining a cheerful resolve.

Femininity

To be a woman is a deep inner calling, a special gift, an ontological voice, to be especially receptive to others. This is the perfection of feminine love. Again, it is a call that is clear to see when the two antitheses of this mode of expressing perfect femininity are seen. The two extremes of feminine receptivity of soul are possessiveness and cold-heartedness.

EXTREME FEMININITY	PERFECT FEMININITY	INADEQUATE FEMININITY
Possessiveness	Receptivity	Cold-heartedness

A woman's receptive biological nature is a good starting point to demonstrate the special gift of women. Having the capacity to welcome life within her own body makes her ever alert to the inner life of others. Before the world knows this new being, the unborn child, she is sensitive to its needs and has hopes for its future. But female persons are much more than biology.

Many people see receptivity (openness or sensitivity) as a weakness, not realising that it is a special strength, a gift that women particularly have to see beyond the exterior and look into the deepest needs of the heart, never separating the inner person from his outward contribution.

This openness–receptivity to others can be employed in the public realm and have an incalculable influence on public policy.

For example, when a female teenager took on the fashion dictates of a giant department store, the store listened to her demand for fashionable clothing that was not sexualised. Also, when women lobby for more humane treatment of prisoners, laws are changed. When women fight against the sex industry's assault on community values, zoning laws change. When women fight against pornography's attack against the value of the human person, public policy follows their lead.

Girls are at the forefront of campaigning against the epidemic of sexual harassment and abuse that occurs in secondary schools. For all too long this has been accepted as "boys will be boys" or "this is just the way things have always been and will always be." This is not so when the power of femininity to be receptive to the cries of their fellow girls who suffer this appalling degradation of their dignity are responded to.

The Church urges women to exercise their receptivity, openness and sensitivity to restore awareness of the humanity of each person. Women can show society, by using their inherent special gift, both in the private and public spheres, how to be receptive to the deepest human needs. It is akin to the maxim that "the person who changes society is the mother who rocks the cradle."

It is a denial of the elephant in the room not to see pregnancy and motherhood both as something unique to women and a lesson provided by the body about the inner nature of women. Pregnancy and motherhood are not just physical realities; they are intensely spiritual. Just go into any antenatal booking clinic and ask the mothers there about what pregnancy means to them. The list is full of spiritual components like dreams, hopes, aspirations and prayers, even the most rudimentary, intensely personal, like "God, if you do exist, look after my child because I am scared", along with the material realities of epidurals, nursery decoration or birthing baths! Male pregnancy and breast feeding are still hopefully an anathema to most people, even though they are logical accompaniments of Gender Ideology.

St John Paul II highlights that receptivity is an essential gift that facilitates women to carry their children within their own body for nine months and nurture them, come what may, for

90 years! He wrote "woman is endowed with a particular capacity for accepting the human being in the concrete form" (37). The concrete form, that is life with all of its ups and downs, is where women are seen as particularly amazing creations! Women, acting as physical or spiritual mothers, remain when the going gets tough.

This singular unique feature, femininity, which prepares her for motherhood not only physically but also emotionally and spiritually, is inherent in the plan of God, who entrusted the care of little dependent human beings to woman in an altogether special way that no man can ever fully replicate.

But receptivity is not all about physical motherhood. If it were, then nuns, unmarried or sterile women would be in some way inferior to their married, childbearing sisters.

Multi-national companies, teaching hospital departments of surgery and Ivy League university professorial chairs need women who are called to this line of work. But they need to be at the top as women who are perfectly feminine, true holistic spiritual mothers in every sphere of human conduct, looking out for those whom they relate to, not adulterated forms of femininity.

Any idea, however, that a stay-at-home mum is less of a woman than a career mum must be opposed. No scientific study can measure the immeasurable benefit to the building blocks of society (children) to a mum who decides this is my calling.

The two extremes that adulterate perfect femininity highlight what women are made to be by enunciating the opposite polarity. They are cold-heartedness and possessiveness.

Inadequate femininity takes the form of cold-heartedness. It is the woman who aspires to be domineering, to be in effect a female-machismo, to be the things that are traditionally ascribed to strong men which are really an insult to perfect masculinity and give credence to the lie that masculinity is better than femininity. It says by the action that women are only as good as men when they behave as men behaving badly.

Cold-hearted women are women acting like bad machismo men! It is a great tragedy because it is a caricature of manhood and a denial of womanhood. It is living a lie. This cold-hearted aggressiveness destroys intimate male–female relationships, makes workplace relationships fraught with distrust and antagonism, and leaves the individual prone to isolation and loneliness. Female power is good when it is used in gentle service. It is to be dreaded when it is used to threaten, dominate or coerce; it makes a woman leader a person to be followed because of fear rather than respect.

Cold-heartedness is a potent destroyer of one-to-one male–female relationships. As the appeal of physical beauty of the female wanes, the aggressiveness can destroy the potential to maintain intimacy because intimacy is "in-to-me-you-see." The belligerent attitude primarily sees the negative points of the person, thus undermining any relationship.

On the other end of the spectrum is extreme femininity. It manifests as possessiveness or vanity. It is harder to spot as it can be masked by all the trappings of stereotypical femininity and what is marketed incorrectly as the perfect woman. It is smothering rather than mothering. The genius of women is to receive the other person and permit them in metaphorical terms the freedom to breathe, the freedom to thrive. If, however, taken to the extreme, the receiving of others holds them to the point of imprisonment so they no longer breathe, they are smothered and their freedom to develop and manifest their gifts is smothered. The desire to control or use others as a possession is immensely damaging to the person themselves and those who relate to them.

Possessiveness is what is called in theological language vanity.

In common parlance "vanity" and "vain" apply to those who are just focused on their looks. But it has a deeper meaning than this; it describes conceited persons with exaggerated self-opinions who show false concern for those with whom they associate and of whom they seek control.

While the theological usage of the word vanity includes this day-to-day nuance of being obsessed with physical beauty, it also describes the world as having no ultimate eternal meaning; others are there just to assist material progress until death ends it all. This theme characterises the Book of Ecclesiastes in the Bible, which begins with the well-known saying "Vanity of vanities! All (without God) is vanity". (38)

Possessiveness manifests in self-adornment, focus on physical appearance, materialistic outlook, an intense sense of self-entitlement, "it is my right" mentality and, of course, being non-receptive, closed to the needs of others despite a superficial concern manifesting frequently as an expansive social network. A vain woman is outwardly well mannered, attractive, apparently attentive to her boyfriend or husband and ready to flatter if it serves a purpose of getting what she wants. It can even be a seductive manipulation. It hurts the woman because the desire to possess and use rather than receive and nurture others is an impossible route to fulfilment since possessiveness can never be satisfied by material possessions or the use of other persons for gratification.

The Equality of Masculinity and Femininity

Masculinity and femininity are two equal but different modes of being. Sadly, the way this was revealed by God in the account of creation in the first book of Genesis has been subjected to many false interpretations that placed women beneath men. St John Paul II explained the correct understanding. (39)

Man (Adam) is made from the earth (adama) but woman is

made from man. Man is just a lump of earth in the poetic language of the author without the creative input of God! But women start their creation from man (a spare rib as the allegorical story goes). This fact that woman is created second does not make her subservient; it is a statement of formation not of purpose.

For woman is not created "second" in purpose; rather she is created last in splendour. And she is, in fact, made on the way up, the last creature to appear, a creature made, not from earth, but from something that arguably already contains a greater beauty than dust or clay. Man is made from the earth, but woman is made from man, better stuff.

The Biblical account strongly says women as a minimum are the equal of men and possibly the pinnacle of creation, not a creature whose place in that order is subservient or somehow less in stature than that of man.

This proposition (but not formal teaching) that woman is formed of finer stuff is reinforced when we consider that the Hebrew word usually translated as "helper" is "ezer" and actually does not mean servant or slave, which it has often been equated to. When this word is used elsewhere in Scripture, it has the connotation of divinely gifted aid. A super gift due to God's generosity to the world would be a modern take on the language.

As much as it is good to praise the wonder of the feminine, care must be taken not to overemphasise that woman is better than man. The full text in the book of Genesis in the original Hebrew language explaining the creation of woman uses the word kekenegdo. Kekenegdo is a preposition that means made "in the sight of". Eve is not "below" Adam in the order of creation, but neither is she above him. The likely meaning is that Eve (the name means woman) stands in front of him, before him, meeting his gaze, equal as it were and sharing in the responsibility to care for creation.

Finally, the concepts of (perfect) masculinity and femininity that men and women are made to be and should strive to be and their extreme antitheses are not six different persons! Everybody struggles to be the sexed person they are meant to be. There is a little bit of Jekyll and Hyde, in varying proportions, in all of us. All men alive today struggle not to be domineering, effeminate or mixtures of both, and all women alive today struggle with the negative connotations of femininity.

Chapter 7

The Reasoned Proof of Binary Gender

For some, it can be difficult to believe that gender is binary, that there are essential innate differences in masculine and feminine that accord to every person on the planet. This is especially true when individuals have not experienced from childhood parents who despite their faults and failings were trying to strive to be the person they were made to be—perfect men and perfect women. This is the primary pedagogy of gender expression, and when adulterations of masculinity and femininity present themselves as the norm, it is perhaps not surprising that the susceptible mind of a child could become confused.

For others, it is as clear as black and white. For some parents, despite concerted efforts to raise a child gender neutral, nature kicks in and they accept defeat! Just looking at the differences of little girls and boys in the playground, mothers and fathers and their parenting techniques, the management style of a good business with happy employees run by a highly respected woman or man, or a million and one other things, says this is in our bones; men are from Mars and women are from Venus, and nobody is from Jupiter!

While the Church can align itself with some of the critiques of socially constructed gender expressions, what may be called accidentals or non-essentials, the Church remains firm in its belief based on reason and divine revelation that everybody is male or female and these names mean something about the intended purpose of life.

For Catholics, the body, and indeed all the material world, is beautiful because it is a gift from God. It is a gift that is full of meaning and purpose, as it teaches how to love others, and how to give to them in a particular mode.

The issue with Gender Ideology is not that it imputes some

socially constructed norms of gender behaviour, but that it permits an individual to escape the real definition of what is gender and what the individual is called to be.

For a Christian truth comes from divine revelation conveyed by Scripture and tradition and from reason. In an age that rejects revelation as a primary source of truth, one is left with reason to refute the argument of transgenderism. To convince atheists of this, let us presume (incorrectly) at this juncture that a human being is made up of just a body and a brain.

Transgenderism believes that a person can really be an individual whose body does not inform who they are. It is a maxim of the ideology that if I say I am a girl, but I was labelled a boy at birth, then I am a girl. Similarly, if I say I am a new third gender, or a 70% boy 30% girl gender and this changes from Monday to Tuesday, then this is true reality. The sincerity of the believers is expressed by the annoyance in those who accept new ideas of gender with the terminology gender reassignment therapies (i.e. hormones or surgery). Quite understandably for them, this is not reassignment (defined as a move or relocation) but should be named gender confirmation (defined as validating the truth) therapies.

But the confirmation of gender divorced from biology and physiology is fiction. Certain therapies attempt to change anatomical and physiological things that can be changed, and then a legal statement is made that this is now a real woman or a real man. But this is nonsense. Why is a real woman made by fashioning an artificial vagina and breasts but does not also involve fashioning the gonads, the minute-to-minute variations in hormone levels, the menstrual cycle, genetic and cellular differences between the sexes, and most importantly pregnancy?

The difference at the genetic and cellular level, the building blocks of biology, cannot be relegated to inconsequential, but transgenderism has to do this to give a credible account.

Approximately 5% of the human genome resides on the X and Y chromosomes—1,846 genes on the X and 454 on the Y. This means that male and female cells are fundamentally dissimilar on a genetic level. (40)

Also, at a cellular level there are profound differences. For example, female neurons (nerve cells) uptake dopamine, a chemical that helps regulate feelings of pain and pleasure, twice as quickly as male neurons. Female neurons and kidney cells are also more susceptible to chemical agents that lead to programmed cell death. And female liver cells contain more of the gene CYP3A. This last difference is especially crucial, as the actions of CYP3A account for the detoxification of many chemicals that are deleterious to cellular health and thus may explain why women on average live longer than men. (41)

Reductio ad absurdum is disproving an argument by showing the ridiculousness of following it through to a logical conclusion. Essentially, the argument is reduced to its absurdity. This works only if there is faulty logic in the argument to begin with. Transgenderism leads to absurdities. Divorce the anatomical signs of masculinity and femininity from the inner reality, and one is left with accepting absurdities like male pregnancy, the male (transplanted) womb and male chest feeders as normality.

A similar absurdity comes with the phenomena of health and disability being the domain of perception rather than bodily reality. These people are known as the transabled. Just as transgender people make a distinction between the sex they were purportedly assigned at birth and the sex they now identify with, the transabled make a distinction between the disabilities of body form society says they don't have and the disabilities they think they have.

Transabled persons have, for example, legs that function properly, but the transabled persons wear leg braces and use wheelchairs, because they identify as "disabled". Living as an able-bodied person is as painful for the transabled person as it is for a transgender person to live in accordance with his or her biological sex. Some transabled persons even ask doctors to help them become disabled (such as by having their spinal cords severed) and they insist their surgery is confirmatory not reassignment or a health-change. (42)

Finally, looking at things from an atheist perspective, according to the theory of materialistic evolution something that is not causally effective cannot lead to evolutionary advantage and cannot be chosen by natural selection. Therefore, there is no evolutionary advantage to transgenderism so it cannot be normative if a person subscribes to the theory of evolution.

Obviously, Catholics are not atheists! Belief in a spiritual reality is the basis of Catholic opposition to transgenderism. When surveys are taken in the Western world asking people if they are religious, there is an increasing majority answering no. But when people are asked "Are you spiritual?", there is an overwhelming positive response. Few people can really believe they are just a bunch of chemicals.

Most people are convinced of their spiritual nature (a soul in religious language). This is because it is an almost inevitable inference from the observed facts of life irrespective of educational achievement, culture, era or location.

The least educated person arrives at the concept of the soul (a spiritual non-material dimension to their being) almost without reflection, certainly without any severe mental effort. The mysteries of birth and death, the lapse of conscious life during sleep and in swooning, even the commonest operations of imagination and memory, which abstract a man from his bodily presence even while awake, the ability to conceptualise things that are not perceived by the senses like God and his or her capacity to appreciate truth, beauty and love, are all beyond physical measurement. There is not 10 inches of beauty or truth! All such facts invincibly suggest the existence of something besides the visible organism, internal to it, but to a large extent independent of it, and leading a life of its own.

For those that do not believe in God, these phenomena are just intricate manifestations of brain function. The mind and the brain are the same thing. But believers in God see the mind (the intellect and the will) as immaterial spiritual entities that need a brain to manifest their presence but are separate from the material brain.

There are many reasons in favour of the soul not being identifiable with the brain. Firstly, to say that if the ability to make free decisions was just a matter of chemicals and electricity, then it becomes a nonsense to impute responsibility. Justice has no meaning. The person may just have had a bad electric day or bad chemical neurotransmitter day. But human beings correctly hold themselves and others accountable for their misdeeds. This is only just if the will is free; that is, it can be judged to be divorced from material (chemical–electrical) constraints.

Also, the proof of the existence of the spiritual component in human beings comes from looking at the intellectual abilities of human beings. The nature of the intellect, its capacity to know abstract things, is a strong indication that the mind (soul) and brain are not the same thing.

St Thomas Aquinas was a world-renowned philosopher alive in the 1200s who has had a profound influence upon Western society to this day. For example, St Thomas's theory of law and justice is the channel through which the accumulated wisdom of Aristotle, the Stoics, Cicero, the Roman Imperial Jurists and St Augustine blended into a rounded was then transmitted to modern times. Thomas's definition and concept of law and its relation to reason and common good clearly underpin our laws in the UK despite ongoing surrendering of protection of the common good to individual choice.

St Thomas Aquinas explained, "The operation of anything follows the mode of its being". (43) A car drives along because its mode of being is to have an internal combustion engine. A bird flies because it has wings. To put it in simple terms, one can tell something of the nature of a thing through examining its actions.

Hence, the spiritual nature of the human intellect can be given credible support through the exhibition of its spiritual power in human acts. One such "spiritual action" that is very difficult to explain by pure physical mechanisms is the power of abstraction.

When a person sees a man he has never met, he sees and perceives a man because he has seen men before. But the person perceives size, colour, weight, smell, etc. From this conglomeration of accidentals, his intellect then abstracts the "form" of "man-ness" from that individual. These are not perceptual things but have their base in things that cannot be measured. The person conceptualises whether he is a rich or poor man, good or bad man, religious or non-religious man, real man or virtual man, etc. If this process was caused by chemical–electrical phenomena and not just mediated by them, then the conclusion would be impossible. This is because anything that is taking place in the brain is known to be an encoded neural firing pattern; certain brain cells do a precise job that is always concrete or specific, as opposed to abstract, the way that a concept is. Thus, the brain is like a radio wave receiver, but the soul (mind) is like a radio wave transmitter. Both are needed to hear the news, but the soul is the transmitter; the means of sound production is the brain.

To reinforce the principle of using abstract thought to show that the mind and brain are different, consider a chiliagon. A chiliagon is a closed regular polygon with 1,000 sides. It is amazingly simple to understand abstractly. However, it cannot be imagined concretely; it is not possible to form a clear picture of a chiliagon in your brain. Thus, abstract thought is not merely an assembly of a large number of concrete thoughts; you do not understand what a chiliagon is simply by imaging a series of many-sided polygons approaching a 1,000-sided figure. (44)

And of course, the biggest abstract thought that is unique to humans is God! No other living being has this capacity.

But arguments from philosophy and neurobiology can never be definitive proof; there will always be debate on these fronts. Catholics believe in the person of Jesus; it is a relationship not a philosophy. Catholics look at the historical evidence that points to the fact he was truly God made man, not just a very good person, so he is worth listening to more than any other person!

Transgenderism holds that a person's sexed body is separate from the being the person really is. It is the intellect, the thoughts, the consciousness that make a person the person that they are. It is summarised in the famous saying "I think therefore I am". (45) It means my conscious thoughts define who I am. This is called dualism (the body is not a pointer to who the person is; it is the conscious thoughts that reveal the person).

There is an atheistic dualism, brain versus body, and a theistic dualism, soul versus brain/body. But the principle is similar. Thoughts define the nature of being; the body does not impart a message about inner reality.

Christian thought believes the opposite aphorism. St Pope John Paul II referred to the great shift in what makes a person. It is not thought which determines existence; rather, existence determines thought! In other words, it is man who thinks, not thinking that makes a man, or to put it simply, *I am therefore I think.* (46) Being (a human) precedes any thoughts. The body serves to inform the nature of the person. So, there are innate qualities like species (no sub-species), body-form (no wings,) body–soul composite (no zombies) and gender (no third or sub-genders)

The proposition that the body and soul are really a composite whole is supported by arguments from reductio ad absurdum; like I may think I am a tree, but my bodily being, which has no leaves or bark, says this is false. It is also supported by the commonly held belief that there are universal inalienable human rights to things like life, nutrition, healthcare and freedom of thought. These rights only have universal validity if the being of the person is inscribed with them; they do not need the validation of the thoughts of the person or indeed another person. Modern-day ideas that give a moral framework to withhold the right to life of the unborn by abortion (47), withhold the right to life of handicapped babies by euthanasia (48) or the demented elderly (49) depend on dualism; the being is not as much of a human person with equal inalienable rights to others because their consciousness is not intact, so their complete personhood comes into question.

It is a truly appalling morality which places personhood and therefore the rights of a person as something acquired not innate. Logically, the more consciousness, the more of a person one becomes by thought. So the professor of astrophysics has more worth than the poor, illiterate, learning-disability, wheelchair-bound child.

Transgenderism is based on the idea that the bodily sexed being does not inform who the person is as thought precedes being. If dualism is true, transgenderism is true. If dualism is not true, then transgenderism is also not true. This question "Does the body inform us about the soul?" has been given a thorough and inciteful interrogation by resorting to reason. (50)

Notice that, as you read this book using the eyes of your body, you sense the words on the page, and at the same time you understand (use your intellect to judge their meaning and importance). It is not as if you understand the words but only your body sees the words.

It is this fact of human experience that led Aristotle in ancient Greece (51) to conclude that the body is not separate from the soul, but they are mixed; the soul in effect extends from the tip of the toe to the tip of the nose. If you are reading ("body-ing") and understanding ("soul-ing") the words, then it necessarily follows that your body is not separate from you. You are not like a car which is separated from a driver, pure dualism. A car has a mechanical form and an intelligent driver, completely separated. But human beings from reason are different. You are not your soul alone, nor are you your body alone, but you are both body and soul that operate as a composite.

Our sexed bodies therefore do matter. If my body and soul together make up the one substance that I am, then it necessarily follows that my male body together with my soul makes me who I am. My male body is not an accident to my personal identity that I can change. My male body is essential to who I am as an individual human person.

It is from such reasoned arguments that Christianity believes in binary gender.

Chapter 8

How Should Persons Who Experience Discordance Between Their Sex and Perceived Gender Be Labelled?

How should a compassionate society label a person who does not feel their biological sex conforms to their gender? Historically, many labels have been used. (Fig. 5)

Fig. 5. The classification of gender

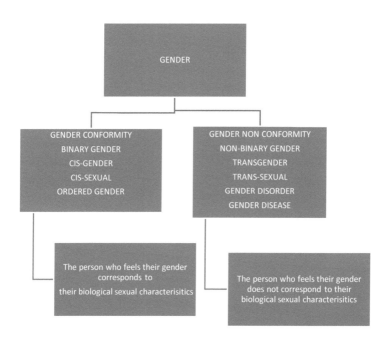

Labels matter because they can be pejorative and can cause great hurt.

Labels are the product of the tendency for human beings to classify things so as to facilitate understanding. There are labels (classifications) for almost everything, be it plants, animals, cars, beauty—the list is endless.

Many people who have a gender sex discordance find the label "disorder" or worse still "disease" very hurtful and not really reflecting how they feel about themselves. The modern label is gender non-conformity. (52)

The critical element of gender non-conformity is the distinction between those individuals who are content with their gender, called gender euphoric, and those that are not, called gender dysphoric. (53)

If Jesus Christ was anything, he was gentle with the vulnerable. Gender non-conforming persons have been the victim of appalling ridicule, violence and ostracisation in the past, and even today there is still a long way to travel.

Therefore, if removing the word disorder or disease takes away a stick to beat these people with, then it can be a good thing. Calling someone mentally disordered is not pleasant. Doctors use harsh language in their professional communications, but quite correctly this should be tempered when pastorally supporting their patients. Gender non-conformity is perhaps a better terminology although even this carries for some a message that is too much to bear.

Chapter 9

Why Does the Church Make Such a Big Deal About Gender Ideology?

Pope Francis has used very strong language to denounce Gender Ideology, equating the evil to a nuclear holocaust. (54) To many it sounds extreme exaggeration. Why would a Pope equate the evil of Gender Ideology to a nuclear holocaust? Why has Gender Ideology been singled out for this degree of warning?

Gender Ideology can seem, at first sight, to be a somewhat irrelevant target because it is clear to the advocates of the ideology, and opponents, that at least in the short- to medium-term only a small minority will succumb to the direct effects of the theory, i.e. question their own binary-assigned gender or seek an anatomical change.

So why does the Church take it so seriously? On a Papal visit to Georgia, the Pope said, in response to a question asked by the local bishops about Gender Ideology: "You mentioned a great enemy of marriage, gender theory." He continued: "Today, there is a global war out to destroy marriage. Not with weapons but with ideas … we have to defend ourselves from ideological colonisation." (55)

In another interview, the strength of the language was also applied to the questioning of gender assignment using the power of exclamation: "Today, in schools they are teaching this to children, to children! That everyone can choose their gender." (56)

And for the Pope the most worrying of all is that the ideology provides the context to doubt the very existence of a personal God who creates good to whom we owe obedience. It is the first and greatest commandment, the primary way we show our love for God.

If seeing the beauty of our bodies should not lead us to use our intellects to find the inner purpose of existence, then there are logical corollaries. All the other beautiful things we see in creation, like trees, oceans, animals and most importantly other people, are logically victim to permitting our intellects to decide to exert an irresponsible domineering dominion (things like abortion, infanticide, euthanasia, environmental degradation and unjust economic systems like liberal capitalism or socialism) rather than a responsible, respectful dominion over beautiful things in creation. Pope Francis said, "Let us not fall into the sin of trying to replace the Creator. We are creatures, and not omnipotent. Creation is prior to us and must be received as a gift." (57)

Despite these things, it can sound reasonable to say something like let them get on with it, leave them alone and let the vast majority carry on as they have since the first man and woman. The Catholic Christian Church refuses to do this because there are direct and indirect effects of the ideology that raise alarm bells where love and justice, gender justice, are seriously threatened.

Direct Effects

1. The ideology gives a framework for a highly damaging corruption of reality for a small but nevertheless highly vulnerable group of people who are supported in their belief that their gender is non-masculine or feminine or not necessarily informed by their biological sex. Jesus had a special love for the vulnerable. So as Catholics we must do likewise.

2. The ideology drives the uptake of medical therapies that are potentially very harmful to the individual. These include hormone manipulations, reassignment surgical procedures and ideas to transplant wombs into men.

Indirect Effects

Ideologies do their main harm by inculcating ideas that take people away from the purpose of their existence. In dictatorships in the 20th century, it resulted in things like Nazism causing violent racism, especially anti-Semitism and violent attacks on people with learning disabilities via state-sponsored forced euthanasia. In Communist ideology, it inculcated violent class hatred, resulting in ferocious destruction of those considered to be obstructing the path to material heaven on earth by mass deportations of innocent middle-class people, killing of aristocratic families including their children and confinement to gulags of hundreds of thousands of innocent people who did not subscribe to the ideology.

In a democracy ideology poisons the purpose of existence by inculcating the ideas that it is choice, consent and tolerance that act as the final arbiters of what gives a human being fulfilment. It is a strategy of moral indifference; there is no objective truth to guide a person. Pope Francis called it "ideological colonisation" where bit by bit false ideas take over the mind of the masses to do in moral terms what physical colonisation did in its historical context, to exploit human persons and lower their dignity. It translates in Gender Ideology to a number of nonsense conclusions from a social science perspective as well as from the revealed truth given by Jesus. If gender does not point to inner realities that tell the purpose of a fulfilled life (it is called teleology), then conclusions are drawn that are erroneous and cause great harm especially to the vulnerable, those with less intellectual abilities or material resources.

These are things like all familial-type relationships being taught as equivalent, and also that marriage is just one choice among many equal choices and gay marriage is the same as heterosexual marriage; no-fault divorce laws undermining the indissolubility of marriage being promulgated as social advances; and sexual intimacy bringing human fulfilment being taught as something that is not related to a heterosexual dyad or a lifelong commitment.

All of these things can be summarised in two detrimental developments:

1. The ideology gives a structure to undermine marriage as an essential part of human nature. By educating that gender is a social construct, then as a logical consequence, marriage is just a social construct, and thus has no more value in terms of human fulfilment than any other intimate relationship. If being a man or a woman means nothing definitive, then the marriage vow "I take this man/this woman as my lawfully wedded wife/husband" means different things to different people; it is a useless piece of paper.

2. The promulgation of the ideology ultimately questions the very existence and nature of a personal God who chose by analogy to reveal himself as a father, or more correctly in etymological terms a daddy. If gender is just an individual perception, and not a fixed reality, then the perception of God as Father/Daddy becomes divorced from any objective reality. If we only owe obedience to our own perception of what our supernatural daddy is, then it becomes a potent route to agnosticism and ultimately atheism. Why bother obeying a God who is a product of perception that can change just like human gender? God can be all good, capricious, divorced from human affairs, a distant dictator. A personal God who has no fixed nature is not worth knowing even if he does exist!

These two facets need to be explored: the effects of undermining marriage and the need for a clear appreciation of gender to establish a relationship with God.

Gender Ideology is very serious because it gives a framework to destroy marriage in the minds of the young. The Church, wanting what is best for human beings, upholds marriage because it is the singular institution that has led over the duration of human history to the best outcomes for children, the parents and society.

This framework for the destruction of marriage was eloquently proposed by Professor Shannon Gilreath, a prominent gender theorist in the USA who honestly communicated:

"The real promise of the transgender movement is not the freedom to figure out ways to become more fully male or fully female, but rather freedom from gender entirely." (58)

From this principle, Professor Gilreath continued to critique the agenda to propose same-sex marriage. He challenges proponents to truly reflect on what there is to commend marriage to gay and lesbian people, and points to his own reversal on the question as evidence.

For Gilreath, the final aim in his analysis is to consign marriage to the history books. Gilreath argues that ultimately marriage should be seen as an unnecessary institutionalisation of gays and lesbians because it is creating new respectable and non-respectable sexualities. It is unintentionally introducing a new injustice. Gays, lesbians and heterosexuals can marry, but a new underclass is created where, for example, bisexuals and polysexuals are excluded from the marriage ticket.

Gilreath concludes by noting that to the extent that marriage is assumed to be normatively good, an equal-access approach to same-sex marriage recognition may be the most successful in the short term, but he invites people to vigorously challenge that assumption of normativity of marriage given the overall premise of gender theory to obliterate gender difference.

Clearly, if there is no essential difference between men and women, then it is absurd to think that such a thing as marriage exists. It becomes a nonsense to believe that the lifelong union of a gender-different man and a gender-different woman can be part of human nature, since if men and women do not exist in reality, then the union of a man and a woman cannot exist. If binary gender is an illusion, then marriage is an illusion, a mere made-up sociological or political institution that has no absolute definition. If one man and one woman are not innately designed to be mutually compatible, a compatibility that is enhanced by lifelong exclusive union, then it is just one of many man-made intimate relationships with no particular advantage to men, women or children. There can be no reason to propose marriage over any other sexually intimate associations such as polyamorous partnerships, peripatetic fathering relationships or dissoluble and conditional cohabitation partnerships (moving-in).

But simply from reason, alternatives to marriage for embarking upon an intimate sexual relationship are clearly not good enough. Many think these alternative options are just as good as it gets due to a loss of confidence in the institution of marriage, but this is not true. Human beings are made for real love that is found in real marriage.

Just imagine the offer of the polyamorous man: "Hi, will you live with me and my other three partners?" Similarly, imagine the offer from a prospective moving-in boyfriend: "Hi, will you live with me? And if I think you are worth it, we can stay together. If not, I shall move on and try someone else." Along the same type of reasoning comes the offer of union from the person where divorce enters the mindset: "Hi, will you marry me until death do us part? I mean, of course, until the death of our relationship, if that should occur before my physical death!" Or the offer from a peripatetic father: "Hi, will you have a relationship with me? But I am not signed up to caring for any children that I sire." And last but most certainly not least, the offer from a woman who is not open to children or a man not prepared to shoulder his responsibilities: "Hi, let us get together, but if pregnancy occurs, then it is time for an abortion as I do not want your children."

Marriage is not a sociological or political construct, or one of many equivalent options. It is very different. The innate gifts of sacrificity of men and receptivity of women are given a pathway to realise this perfection in marriage which facilitates real love. Human beings are made for love. Ask a person who is called to marriage why they feel this way. The answer is not because the Prime Minister, President, an academic department of sociology at Oxford University or indeed the Pope made an institution that they suggest a couple should sign up to! Rather, it is because there is a deep inner calling that this will change the person for the better, to be a true lover.

Marriage is not like joining the local tennis club where one takes a look at the rules and regulations, the benefits and the costs and then says yes or no. That is a social construct. The call to marriage is in the heart, what is called ontological, written in our nature.

Marriage is an inner call that is marked by desires to express affinity, reciprocity, complementariness, exclusivity, indissolubility, procreativity and unconditionality. (Fig. 6) It is a way that the design of men to sacrifice themselves for the wellbeing of another and the design of women having the unique sensitivity to accept another person despite their faults and failings can find a place where these geniuses can be mutually beneficial and thus help the couple to flourish.

From antiquity, monogamous lifelong union was proposed but most certainly was not the normative practice in the pre-Christian world. Polygamy and desertion along with appalling sexual violence towards women were common. Jesus really changed the world for the better. It was not reason and science that civilised male–female intimacy. It was Christianity converting barbarian men into knights in shing armour. And it was marriage that was the means of this amazing transformation. Eminent secular Oxford university historians agree! (59)

Fig. 6 The meaning of marriage

INNER (ONTOLOGICAL) CALL TO MARRIAGE	WHAT THE HEART IS SAYING
Affinity	"I want to be with you"
Reciprocity	"I know I can be good for you"
Complementariness	"I know you and I together will always make something bigger than both of us just added together"
Exclusivity	"I want only you"
Indissolubility	"I want to be with you always until I die"
Procreativity	"I would like to see another you in the world"
Unconditionality	"I want to give you my all"

So, what is marriage? There are only two possible kinds of answers to this question: either marriage and family have a fixed, natural (in our bones) purpose (teleology) and inner nature (ontology), or they do not. If not, marriage is some kind of social construction, an invention of culture like a club with rules that can change over time.

It is not culture that constructs marriage and family. Rather, it is the other way around: marriage and the thing it makes called family construct culture. As the building blocks of civilization, families are logically prior to society as the parts are prior to the whole. Bricks are not the result of the building, because the building is made up of bricks. You must have the first before you can get the second.

Societies are large groups of families. Since families are constituent of culture, cultures cannot define them. They merely observe their parts, as it were, and acknowledge what they have discovered. Society then enacts laws not to create marriage and families according to arbitrary convention, but to protect that which already exists, being essential to the whole.

Why has civilization always characterised families as a union of men and women as being the norm? Because men and women are the natural source of the children that allow civilized culture to persist. Marriage begins a family. Families are the building blocks of cultures. Families and therefore marriages are logically prior to culture.

Families, defined as a man and a woman in lifelong union, may fail to produce children, either by choice, age or accident, but they are about children, nonetheless because they signal this is how we generate family and build society.

This rendering of the lived reality of marriage into nonsense by accepting Gender Ideology was put aptly by J K Rowling, the author of the Harry Potter stories. The reality of the millions of women who live as mothers and wives becomes shattered if Gender Ideology is adopted as being true. She tweeted: "If sex (i.e. pointing to binary gender) isn't real, the lived reality of women globally is erased. I know and love trans-people but erasing the concept of sex removes the ability of many to meaningfully discuss their lives. It isn't hate to speak the truth." (60)

The effect of adopting Gender Ideology as a real phenomenon on religious belief is the other potent reason the Pope is concerned.

There is a need for a clear appreciation of what gender really is to establish a relationship with God. This is because the knowledge of the love of God in Christian theology is intricately tied up with gender-specific familial terminology. God chose this way to educate human beings about his nature by using the word Father (Daddy) as his title.

God as a spirit has no body and therefore no gender. He is beyond our complete comprehension. But the earthly language that presents a picture to us of God in the Bible is tied in with the analogy (close comparisons with real similarities) of fatherhood as well as metaphors (comparisons that have no direct link but make the message clear by non-real comparisons) of fatherhood and motherhood.

It is not just the flick of the coin, heads or tails, why God asked us to address him as Father and not Mother, or a choice people can make. Mothers and fathers share many features in common in terms of relationship with their children. However, a father is different from a mother in our earthly existence because a father creates and sustains children outside of himself whereas a mother creates and nurtures within herself (we call it pregnancy). This father analogy of God is called being transcendent.

This separation of creation from the creator is very important as it defines God as being greater than any created thing. Man has a tendency to limit God, to have multiple competing gods like power, sex, money and fame, to make God an irrelevancy in day-to-day life, to make a god (an all important thing) out of a mere created thing like recycling rubbish or saving the tiger from extinction, or to see God as an equal fighter between evil and good spirits. Being transcendent means that he exists both above and independently from all creation. He is number truly one! And the word father has to mean something if this pedagogy has any resonance.

In other words, there is nothing that matches his power to bring true joy. He is not a divine person with a need to be praised for his own sense of worth. God has no need of it. He is perfectly happy; he seeks praise as a gift to us, to reassure us that all things will work out well if we love God. Praise and worship are divine life insurance policies.

In addition, nothing else can interfere with his power. He created all space, time, energy and matter. Therefore, he is able to control all things as he pleases. He is therefore the one to follow and adore. He is our Father, a word that means something, our transcendent all-loving Master.

God is shown to be remarkably close to us by using metaphorical terms like a mother suckling her child or like a father being a rock to resist adversity. Nothing is impossible for God; any adverse situation can be a pathway to a deep faith. No family alive is perfect. Many saints had objectively disastrous familial starts. But the example of a loving father and mother to children is the primordial pedagogy for the appreciation of the intense love God has for the human person and nurturing faith.

Without this experience, it is a more difficult process for the seed of faith in God to flourish. This is demonstrated by looking at the intergenerational transmission of faith. There is clear correlation with family integrity and negative correlation with family rupture, and most importantly fathers not doing their bit. For example, a rather obscure, but an exceptionally large, academically robust and important study conducted by the Swiss government revealed some astonishing facts with regard to the generational transmission of faith and the importance of fathers. (61) It is 20 years old and probably the results have deteriorated in terms of religious practice, but the principle still stands.

In short, the study showed that if a father lives his faith regardless of the practice of the mother, about two-thirds of their children will become churchgoers. In contrast, a non-practising father with a practising mother will see two-thirds of his children never darken the church door. Worse still, a single abandoned mother (where the rupture of day-to-day fatherly love is complete) who tries her best to transmit faith has only a 2% chance of seeing her children adopt a significant role for religion in their lives.

To be scientifically correct, these are correlations not proven causations. There are, of course, subsets. St Martin de Porres had an abandoned single mum! It may be that it is not fathers or mothers themselves, but the socio-economic, educational or cultural differences associated with these family breakdowns that are the real cause of the diminution of faith. But against this, the Swiss work looked at the whole population, so the direct family structure on the balance of probabilities seems the most likely root cause.

The results are shocking, but really, they should not be surprising. They are about as politically incorrect as it is possible to be, but they simply confirm what psychologists, criminologists and educationalists know: that dads matter and that having a mum and dad at home who love each other matters. The best thing parents can do for their children is to love each other and both to love God with all of their hearts.

Just from common knowledge, leaving sociological studies out of the mix, nobody is really surprised that if a child has a mother who abuses and neglects him or her, or a father who is more interested in looking for a new girlfriend than caring for his wife and child and leaves home, the metaphors and analogies used to imprint the idea of a loving God do not resonate as well in the young mind of the child. These brain connections persist into adulthood with the predictable results in terms of faith.

Neurobiological and psychological insights into effective parenting conclude, not surprisingly, that parents need to be unconditionally available, responsive and sensitive to the needs of their children to ensure all manner of positive outcomes in child rearing. (62) For those who believe in God, a key positive endpoint is love for God!

Therefore, protection of marriage and family faith-filled living are critically important for Christians to facilitate. Any assault, be it the promulgation of Gender Ideology or things like open marriages, adultery, divorce or unjust economic systems that do not offer access to a family living wage and thus can contribute to family breakdown are vigorously opposed.

In summary, as indirect effects Gender Ideology is causing an "educational crisis" because it is being taught to children. (63) The crisis in the eyes of the Church has the potential to undermine family and faith. To some, this can sound exaggerated nonsense. It is contended that Gender Ideology is just an opportunity to educate the young as one option then leave it up to them to decide. The idea being, we only inform; we do not propose.

But this is not true. Teachers have a profound influence on children; what comes out of their mouths is commonly presumed to be true. Children rarely possess skills of critical appraisal. Also, it is untrue because nobody would dream of just educating or informing about the Holocaust as an historical event without ensuring the pupils believed it was a vital lesson about the errors of anti-Semitism. Similarly, health education is predicated on communicating ways to avoid harm, not just informing pupils about the variety of illicit drug syndromes, sexually transmitted diseases and mental health threats. The same standard is required to rebut Gender Ideology.

Chapter 10

What Causes Gender Non-Conformity?

If one accepts that gender non-conformity is a condition that can be placed into a medical model of seeking a cause (something strongly contested by some of those who see it as a primarily simple learned variable in the human condition), then the table below (Fig. 7) summarises the current state of knowledge.

The table cites the scientific references for those who wish to explore the meaning of the medical terminology in greater depth and the theoretical background of the postulated causes.

Many scholars of Gender Ideology, and transgender people themselves, understandably contest the very rationale of searching for a cause of transgenderism. An assumption behind this quest for a cause is that gender dimorphism (the idea that there are only two discrete, well-defined genders) is an established fact, which is the very point of contention.

This is the big debate. Is gender primarily a blank sheet of paper that is written as life goes on, or is it a pre-prepared script that can be influenced by the events of life? The former view is called behaviourism, also known as behavioural psychology. It is a theory of learning which states all behaviours are learned through interaction with the environment through a process called conditioning or rehearsal. Performatism is one such behavioural theory.

Conditioning is the learning process in which the likelihood of a specific behaviour increases or decreases in response to reinforcement or punishment that occurs when the behaviour is exhibited, so that the subject comes to associate the behaviour with the pleasure from the reinforcement or the displeasure from the punishment.

The new ideas about gender usually place gender identity into this mindset. Gender is primarily something that is done. It is primarily achieved rather than innate; it is part of a collective endeavour, not an individual odyssey.

When seeking a cause for gender non-conformity, it is important to state that this is a very unclear area of research. Idiopathic cause (unknown) or multifactorial (many occurring synchronously) are probably the commonest most likely diagnoses. The transgender experience is diverse and varied. A gender non-conforming person can be someone who believes they are a male in a female body or a female in a body that has no gender or maybe changes from day to day. It seems unlikely that a one-size-fits-all explanation is tenable.

A transgender person can overlap with intersex conditions, have contrasting sex chromosomes, genitalia, brain sex, hormone levels, and psychological dispositions, making it difficult to clearly decide whether that person is male or female. A diagnosis of uncertain gender is sometimes a valid diagnosis in this situation. This does not mean that male and female do not exist, but it does mean that this distinction can at times be ambiguous and unclear in certain individuals.

Obviously, theoretically gender identity can be an arbitrary preference. We can all decide to identify as anything we want to identify with. But gender is usually not simply about arbitrary preference, and it would be both disparaging towards the individual and scientifically reckless to assume this in any individual who does not volunteer this information.

The psychological postulated causes of gender non-conformity opposing behavioural psychology come under the heading of cognitive psychology. The main difference between behaviourism and cognitive psychology is that, in behaviourism, human behaviour is decided by the experiences one has had as consequences of various similar actions whereas cognitive psychology is based on the fact that humans have the capability to process and analyse various information in their mind.

Most individuals who experience gender non-conformity have no clear genetic or neuro-biological deficits. Similarly, they have the same anatomy and physiology as people who conform to sex and gender synchrony. Therefore, a prominent psychological theory for why people experience gender non-conformity is the psychological process called dissociation.

Dissociation is a psychological experience in which people feel disconnected from their sensory experience, sense of self or personal history. It is usually experienced as a feeling of intense alienation or unreality, in which the person loses their sense of things like what they are, where they are, who they are, what they are doing. It is triggered by traumatic life events. These events are sometimes difficult to ascertain and are deep in the subconscious.

In terms of gender non-conformity, numerous triggers have been postulated, e.g. parents wanted the opposite sex, sexual trauma, fear of assault and being bullied when a girl has facial features and body habitus that look more stereotypically male and vice versa for boys, but none have proven definitively to make the person believe their gender is incongruent with their anatomical sex.

In summary, seeking a cause is often an essential part of the therapeutic strategy to help individuals suffering gender dysphoria.

Postulated selected non-behavioural causes of gender non-conformity

Primary Isolated Phenomena

Secondary As Part of a Known Disease Process

Neuro-Biological Causes
1. Intersex-Overlap Conditons (64)
2. Damaged "Gender" Brain Structure (65)
3. Chimerisation (66)
4. Intrauterine Sex Hormone Timing Dysynchrony (67)
5. Genetic Damage (68)

1. An Epiphenomenon of Mental Illness (69)
2. Drug Exposures (70)
3. Personality Mental Disorders (71)

Cognitive Psychological Causes
1. Dissociation (72)
2. Contagion (73)
3. Factitous (74)
4. Preference/Fluidity (75)

Chapter 11

How to Tell If the Person Is a Boy or a Girl

The history of "science" is full of widows. This means that what was considered to be certain by most intelligent people in one age was later on found out to be incorrect or needed further nuanced clarification. Just think about things like the sun revolving around the earth and then Copernicus changed all that, infections being caused by internal bad "miasma" not external germs which Pasteur discovered or blood being generated and consumed not circulated around the body as William Harvey demonstrated. Also, the speed of progress working out the role of the human genome should make everybody stand back with a degree of circumspection. (76) Many eminent scientists counsel caution in interpreting the science of today as the truth of tomorrow. (77)

In the Catholic view, original sin damaged human beings in ways known and unknown. Original sin was a choice made by our first parents to either follow God or make their own rules. A bad choice led to the damage of human nature in many ways.

It is theoretically possible (though not proven) that a person was ontologically male but succumbed to such damage from original sin that all of the currently known biological pointers present in the individual who has not reproduced shout female!

The only 100% certainties about human being identity are revealed truths. These are:

1. All beings conceived from human gametes (sperm and/or ova) are human beings. As Scripture says poetically, make human beings from your gametes, "be fruitful and multiply". There are no semi-humans; it is all or none. (78)

2. All human beings have a body and a soul; there are no

zombies, bodies with no souls. Repeatedly in Scripture, people are referred to as having "souls" and being embodied "souls". Jesus said we were "not to fear men, who can only kill the body, but not the soul." (79)

3. All human beings are made male or female; there are no third, fourth, fifth, etc. genders. (80)

When these revealed truths are assimilated, the following conclusion can be made: a person who naturally fathers a child is a man made of a body and an immortal soul. Likewise, a person who naturally becomes pregnant is a woman made of a body and an immortal soul. In these cases, biology accords with revelation so it can be believed unreservedly without worrying about the unreliability of science.

From looking at biology alone, the Catholic Church does not know if gender discordance in any specific person is genetic, hormonal or acquired from the environment or a mixture of everything. It is outside of the competence of the Catholic Church to decide. The Church only claims infallibility in matters of faith and morals.

So human beings need to use their intelligence to decipher who is a boy and who is a girl at birth. Objective biological realities are the best option we have, or else nothing is real. If feelings are the number-one criterion on which to base judgement about the world around us, then trees can become cars, lions become ducks and mums become dads at the whim of a thought!

Perhaps the best scientific way that biological reality is appraised by the intellect is called systems analysis. By using systems analysis, we can be confident of getting it right something like 99.9 times of 100 and be humble enough to know that occasionally a painful mistake can be made. But hard, painful cases cannot be used to make definitive judgements else we are subscribing to an inverted, absurd systems analysis, using the odd thing to judge normality. (81)

So, what is systems analysis? (82) In biological and indeed non-biological systems, we gain insight to what they are by looking at both structure and function.

The most common day-to-day view of what makes a human being is to see the human being as a collection of organs that summate to form the macro-structure of being. "He looks like a man, etc.": a (macro) structural approach.

Another approach is to see the body as an organised collection of different kinds of cells, such as nerve cells, heart cells or skin cells, just to name a few of over 200 cell types in the human body, all working together in the organic whole: a (macro) functional approach. But neither alone is reliable. There are lots of humans with no eyes (structure), and there are lots of humans who cannot walk (function).

The more radical perspective of defining what is human and what is a male or female human is offered by systems analysis. This is to see the human organism male and female as a dynamic, complex and seamlessly integrated network of the lowest common denominator of structure and functions. So, the structure and function relates not only to organs nor even to cells but also to molecules, including DNA, RNA, lipids and proteins, connected by reaction pathways which generate the functions of life. In terms of gender, the most reliable (micro and macro) structure and function system is the capacity to father or mother a child. Everything comes together perfectly, from sexual organ structure, sexual intercourse, gametes, intracellular processes of cell replication, all the way down to tiny parts of the DNA, etc. – a full system in action! This provides the greatest certitude from reason of gender, and since it accords with a revealed truth (humans only reproduce male and female humans), it is 100% true.

If this systems approach placing actual motherhood and

fatherhood or potential motherhood or fatherhood as definitive biological proofs of female and male gender is abandoned, then the terms mother and father must be abandoned. Gender Ideologists freely admit this and indeed campaign for the abolition of mother and father on the grounds of discrimination against those who express gender non-conformity. (83) Hopefully, most people can still see this is just nonsense.

The time is fast approaching when by a combination of IVF, womb transplant, specialised drugs to prevent rejection of the womb but not the pregnancy and intricate use of hormone medication a male shall become pregnant! This is not a proof of gender fluidity but a proof of the capacity of man to abuse freedom. Freedom is meant to be free to choose what is best, not free to do what one likes. The latter permits all manner of Frankensteinian aberrations of the human form to be contemplated. The destructive effects upon the child who may be the result of this experiment should counsel against this, but it is not looking hopeful at this point in history!

It is a religious obligation to use reason to the best of our ability since it is one way God wants us to understand the beauty of creation and thus be drawn to worship the creator. (84)

The degree of biological certitude about gender identity becomes less certain as the system analysed becomes less integrated. Thus, moving down the spectrum of certitude about gender assignment, chromosomes, genes, hormones, functional gametes and sex organ structure and function provide greater certitude in predicting gender than, say, big muscles, hairy legs or little breast tissue. There are a lot of real men who are skinny, hairless and sport large breasts! Similarly, gender expressions like "tomboy girls", "boys like guns", "girls like dolls" or "girls prefer perfume" have minimal biological predictive value. It is why the midwife or birth attendant looks at the genitals and then shouts, "It is a boy" or "It is a girl." The midwife or birth attendant are applying systems biology in the best way that she or he can, given the evidence presented.

Finally, part of systems analysis is a bit of philosophy called phenomenology. (85) It provides a means of rapprochement towards the new Gender Ideologists. St Pope John Paul II was a Professor of Philosophy subscribing to phenomenologist ideas. He considered that the reasoned evidence suggests that the personal experience of something always should be considered as part of the picture to what that thing really is.

Someone who had the objective male body but lacked a proper male experience of his body would not, in the eyes of St John Paul II, have the fullness of masculinity or male sex/gender. By the same logic, given that it is possible to have female experience without an objectively female body, true femininity and the female sex/gender would not be present.

But for St John Paul II, a physically male person can never be said in any meaningful sense to be female, as the non-damaged female body is essential from reason to being female as per systems analysis. On the other hand, saying that such a person is entirely male, full stop, no qualification, is inaccurate because the experience of masculinity is essential to being male. A real male but a damaged male would be a description of such a person, not, as a Performatist would say, a female or some other invented gender in a male body.

Chapter 12

Ethical Treatment Options for Gender Dysphoria

Gender dysphoria is a serious condition. It can lead to death by deliberate self-harm. Many studies put the lifetime risk of suicide > 40% in those who suffer gender dysphoria; this compares to < 2% in the general population. (86) All agree something must be done!

In any discussion about treatment, the first thing that must be confronted is the use of emotion to cloud proper scientific thinking.

Given the risk to life, the options about treatment are frequently posed as the emotionally charged and biased dyad of immediate compassionate affirmation of the desire to undergo medical or surgical procedures designed to alter the body form versus immediate compulsory ratification of the assigned gender at birth. (86) The latter option sounds cruel and heartless, so not surprisingly the first option gets airplay and makes headline news.

Also, it is emotionally powerful but scientifically naive to cite an individual purporting everything is now fine, or so much better since surgery was performed, to justify "sex change" treatments or just say the proof is to agree with the person who had this treatment as this is their choice and that is the primary consideration. (87) It is very well known that looking at a large sample of people receiving any treatment over short-, intermediate- and long-term periods is the only safe way to make scientifically robust conclusions about safety and efficacy. The list of biases seriously distorting the conclusions that results from looking at one individual or just a few individuals is enormous. It includes sample size bias, mixed sampling bias (gender non-conformity is unlikely to be the same process in all individuals), social desirability bias and reporting bias to name just a few. Also, many long-term population studies show negligible differences in satisfaction scores when treatment is given or not given and large numbers of patients seek to reverse surgery that was performed on them.

But there is a third way to treat! Pope Francis calls it "accompaniment". (88) It means to gently help any person who is suffering a moral dilemma to see the truth about what is best for them over a period by patiently being available, responsive and sensitive to their needs. It is being a long-term, through-the-ups-and-downs lover. Love is not licence. True love involves justice, *Gender Justice*; it means sometimes saying yes and sometimes saying no according to what is best. At the heart of this is mercy. Mercy is not saying doing wrong does not matter. Doing bad things harms self, damages others and offends God, who sees his children in pain. Mercy is saying doing x is not good but I am here to help you change; I am with you as a companion, a fellow person who travels alongside who also needs mercy. It is an offer to improve, not an offer to remain the same. Real mercy thus has justice (improvement or correction) not licence (you choose and that is the right thing to do) at its heart.

Since to love someone is merciful justice, the question that must be asked is, what is real justice? Justice has a variety of meanings in our world. There is what may be called the "left-wing" view that justice is the greatest good for the greatest number, the collective good. Alternatively, justice may entail the "right wing" view that justice is the greatest good for the individual, the individual good. The Christian view is that the highest justice seeks to uphold the rights of the most vulnerable over and above the more powerful, the common good. It is usually expressed as seeking to support those most in need or looking out for the underdog. Sometimes the most vulnerable will be the person suffering gender dysphoria but sometimes not!

The treatment options may be classified into two groups:

Group 1: Generally accepted ethically approved interventions.

1. Particularly in the young, where about 80% spontaneously recover from gender dysphoria, it is considered best by many respected clinicians to try to minimise the reinforcement of the dysphoria and offer comforting support as things hopefully resolve over time. This is the policy of the National Health Service in the UK. The usual pathway for children and teenagers involves things like family therapy, individual child psychotherapy, parental support or counselling, group work for young people and their parents, regular reviews to monitor gender identity development and/or referral to a local Children and Young People's Mental Health Services for more serious emotional issues. (89)

2. Seeking and treating any recognised disease process that may have the symptom of gender dysphoria.

3. Sometimes simple behavioural changes assuage the ideas of self-harm that can overwhelm persons who suffer gender dysphoria. For example, if a man wants to use make-up, sport earrings, walk in high heels, wear dresses, opt for pink, have hair down to their waist, play netball, enjoy embroidery and aspire to a career which currently has a female predominance, these things cannot be construed in themselves as sinful.

In the Catholic view, the former conclusion is conditional that these expressions are done to help psychological distress. They should not be done for a damaging motive like encouraging inappropriate sexual advances, to cover up a desire for effeminacy, to offend others, to seek sexual intimacy, to militantly project a false ideology of gender or to challenge reasonable rules of modesty where modesty is seen as behaviours (not just clothes covering erogenous zones) that protect the individual from the devaluation of being regarded as a mere object for the sexual gratification of others.

4. Name change, John to Sarah, or Sarah to John. Addressing

the person by their chosen name can be a simple way to help the person who suffers gender dysphoria cope on a day-to-day basis. Names are gender neutral. For example, many girls and boys are called Charlie, many priests co-opt Mary into their name and there are quite a few Sister Joseph nuns in existence. The vast majority of names are a social construct. For example, Sarah is currently a girl's name in the UK; it could be chosen to be a boy's name in the future. This happens over time; for example, Charlie is now an accepted girl's name despite being a derivative of Charles. There are numerous other examples.

5. Trying to educate others, especially those in close contact like family, work colleagues and friends, to be supportive and understanding and not to ridicule, persecute or be violent towards those who challenge stereotypical ideas of gender. This education sadly may be required in Catholicism so as the gender non-conforming individual is truly integrated into the parish and not made to feel a second-class Catholic.

6. Psychoeducational counselling can be helpful for some adults.

7. Actively monitoring for the development of depression, which can be treated with the appropriate psychological or pharmacological tools. This must include regular assessment of the mental state of the person to try to pick up signs of imminent deliberate self-harm so as timely preventative intervention can occur.

Group 2. Controversial interventions that are contested on medical or moral grounds.

1. Surgery and drug therapies are offered to many people who suffer gender dysphoria to effect what is called gender reassignment or gender confirmation. They are commonly called sex-change operations, sex-change medications or together Transition-Related Medical Interventions (TRMIs).

They alter the body form to appear more like the stereotypical appearance of the gender the person believes that they are meant to be.

There are medical and moral reasons why these therapies are disputed to be in the overall best interests of the patient.

Firstly, on medical grounds, performing therapies just because a patient feels they want something done without regard to the harm they can cause is medically suspect. The first principle of the Hippocratic Oath is "first do no harm."

In terms of hormone therapy, some research tends to support the evidence that hormone therapy reduces symptoms of anxiety and dissociation, lowering perceived and social distress and improving quality of life and self-esteem in those who suffer gender dysphoria. (90) However, the research is far from perfect because it is almost impossible to exclude confounding factors. These are things that the patients experience alongside the hormone treatment that may be the real cause of their perceived improvement in distress.

Specific confounders included the following factors, which could impact the mental health of participants independently of hormone therapy: receiving psychotherapy in addition to hormone therapy, accessing other medical gender affirmation technologies (i.e. silicon injections, surgeries, electrolysis) in addition to hormone therapy, possessing any underlying treated or untreated comorbid psychiatric conditions, relationship factors and social support (positive or negative relationships with family, friends or spouse), discrimination experiences (in employment, housing, etc.), barriers and facilitators to healthcare access, prior or concurrent use of street-based hormones, and patient characteristics (age, income, level of education) to name just a few.

Also, any benefits in mental health have to be balanced against very dangerous and potentially life-threatening health implications that have been uncovered concerning the administration of hormone treatments. As treatments go, hormone therapy is relatively safe; it would be disingenuous to suggest otherwise. Also, it is impossible to prove that there may be a direct mortality effect of the hormones because of confounding factors such as suicide, AIDS-related diseases, substance abuse and de novo heart disease. But it is certainly possible.

Hormones are certainly known not to be completely safe. For example, the risk of heart attacks is at least doubled. (91) Therefore, the question must be asked, why risk the physical health and maybe the life of a patient? The answer offered is because the patient feels this is what is best, but that is the essence of the debate: what is truly best?

Perhaps the key medical question is what are the effects of so-called TRMIs in terms of suicidal ideation and completion compared to non-Transition-Related Medical Interventions (n-TRMIs)?

The evidence as it stands is far from robust. n-TRMIs have not been studied in a universally accepted, valid medical trial to see how they compare to TRMIs in terms of suicide risk. It is an impossible trial to perfect because of confounding factors, not least of which are that the label transgender is probably a label that encompasses numerous different types of processes resulting in the thought that gender is different to sex, and follow-up of patients is notoriously difficult. The list of other confounders is also immense, including the different psychology that makes one person opt for TRMI and another otherwise identical person opt for non-TRMI, socio-economic status, social network support, educational achievement and the ability of the person to pass as the opposite sex in a public arena. Also, attempted suicide and completed suicide are sometimes two distinct populations.

The biggest study trying to look at surgery is now over 10

years old. A 2011 long-term follow-up study from Sweden found that sex reassignment was not efficacious, because after sex reassignment, transgender individuals had higher risks of psychiatric morbidity, suicidal behaviour and mortality overall than the general population, when using controls of the same birth sex. The study concluded that 'sex reassignment' may alleviate 'gender dysphoria' but 'may not suffice as treatment for transsexualism" in terms of suicide risk. (92) The bottom line is that nobody really knows the answer because of methodological flaws, and it is just bad science on either side of the debate to invoke infallibility and say the evidence is clear.

This is one good reason why, if the absolute values possibly suggest that life is not being saved, many doctors would invoke the Hippocratic principle and say "No!" This is not because sometimes doctors and patients reasonably decide together to risk life to try to cure an illness but this is done weighing the pros and cons, looking at the alternatives and ensuring the conscience of the doctor is convinced this is a good thing to do. This is good medicine.

Following on from this thought process, for many conscientious doctors the type and reliability of outcome data for TRMIs that is published makes the option of advising TRIMs questionable in terms of the sensible appraisal of the literature. For example, it is often reported that recent evidence strongly suggests sex reassignment surgery is successful. This type of statement is powerful propaganda. The advocates say that regret is rare, and that 98 percent of surgeries are successful. While the figure is true for surgical complications, before anybody accepts a narrative of surgical success equalling holistic success, we should consider the evidence. To evaluate success or failure, we need to go beyond the mechanical skill of the surgeon and to examine the emotional and psychological wholeness of the patient afterwards—and not just in the first few months, but in the years to come.

This is where the problem starts. Most people do not realize that the outcomes of all sex transition procedures are not tracked over time with great precision. This is not because of not trying but because it is a notoriously difficult thing to do. Therefore, no one on either side of the argument knows definitively for example how many people are happy, how many have regrets, how many return to their birth sex, or how many have died because of suicide. When studies are conducted, the results are often based on a minority of the participants because of the lost to follow up rate. This is the number of patients who cannot be traced following their treatment so their outcomes are not known. This introduces a bias into the results. Social acceptability (desirability) too can potentially create bias in such studies.Social acceptability bias can imply admitting regrets is seen as a traitor to the cause, so the reported happiness with all treatments performed needs to be taken with a degree of circumspection. This inevitably raises a question mark regarding over-confident statistics such that a person familiar with critiquing scientific papers finds it difficult to unreservedly believe them.

Leaving aside medical objections, the important discussion is, can these treatments ever be morally correct if they were safe and effective in the desire to prevent suicide?

While it is true to say that the teaching authority of the Catholic Church, known as the Magisterium, has never formally condemned TRMIs, there is formal condemnation of mutilation. (93) Any mutilation performed on innocent people without it being a foreseen but unintended proportionate side effect is immoral. So, for example, while amputation of a cancerous limb or a circumcision is licit because they are judged necessary to prevent disease, cutting off a healthy arm for a transabled person because they feel they are meant to be a one-armed person or the penis of a transgender person because they feel they are meant to be a woman is considered to be illicit. Also, rendering a person infertile when this is a known and intended act has always been taught as illicit.

However, the case is a little more nuanced in gender non-conformity. The desperate plight some transgender persons feel at the sight of a non-congruent body with their perceived gender means that, to preserve them from thoughts of self-harm and suicide, possibly the only way to help a specific individual is to refashion the body form subtlety by drugs, cosmetic injections or surgery. This may be framed as a therapeutic body image adjustment (a psycho-adjustment therapy) rather than a mutilation.

The Church has not declared itself on this question because it is almost an impossible question to answer. What is proportionate? For example, some patients with a very low dose of hormone therapy have minimal overt change (mutilation) in body form, can still regain their fertility at a future date and obtain immense psychological relief, so is this intervention a primary mutilation or primary psychiatric intervention with a recognised but undesired side effect by the doctor of mutilation? This is called Low Dose Gender Affirming Hormone Therapy (LD-GAHT.) The conscience of the patient and the doctor may in the final analysis be the best arbiter. Sometimes we have to say that we do not have all the answers to moral conundrums as clear objective statements.

Also, in Catholic eyes, sexual difference touches very much upon various non-genital—as well as genital—aspects of embodiment. Masculinity and femininity are primarily metaphysical attributes. Hence the question of determining gender and how to integrate this gender into life can become quite complicated. Given the magnitude of the damage done by original sin, it is theoretically possible (though not proven) that for some, "brain sex" may be closer to a person's ontological gender than, say, an infertile genital-gonad defined sex where actual or potential parenthood is not possible so that the definitive proof of certitude of gender (fathering or mothering a child) cannot be cited.

In the Catholic view, the transgendered person is one who most probably suffers a disorder of "assumption" like those in other disorders familiar to psychiatrists. With the transgendered, the disordered assumption is that the individual differs from what seems given in nature—namely one's maleness or femaleness. Other kinds of disordered assumptions are held, for example, by those who suffer from anorexia and bulimia nervosa, where the assumption that departs from physical reality is the belief by the dangerously thin that they are overweight. These diseases carry a high suicide risk score, but nobody would commonly contemplate liposuction in the therapeutic regimen! This type of thought process needs to go on to prevent ideological poisoning corrupting the common sense of the doctor.

It is possible that a mistake is made about ontological reality using the body to decide, but the alternative strategy of permitting a denial of visible embodiment as the means to inform about gender is very dangerous territory for those that want to do the most amount of good. This is because it is likely to be a failure to use our intelligence to the best of our ability; it enters the realm of absurdity, and statistically speaking, the chance of making an error is increased because there are no objective markers of "brain sex" to measure against. To love somebody is to use our talents, in this case our intellects, to serve their wellbeing to the best of our ability.

Thus, the common conclusion regarding TRMIs is to avoid any drugs or surgery that would destroy fertility and/or significantly alter body form since this is likely to be harmful to the true identity of the person. A doctor may occasionally be left with the humble conclusion "I do not know what your ontological gender is but this is the best I can do to ascertain it". Uncertain gender is a real albeit rare possibility in a world that has had the consequences of the original sin of the first man and woman thrust upon it.

Treatment is a particularly very sensitive and painful subject for the parents of children suffering gender dysphoria. The Church extends her pastoral care especially to those parents whose children suffer gender dysphoria. Parents in such situations experience a profound sorrow as they witness their children's suffering. Their sorrow is often deepened if their children individually pursue radical "gender affirming" therapy, which is a harmful and life-altering path against their wishes.

In difficult circumstances, parents are often tempted to think that their Catholic faith is at odds with what is good for their child. In fact, authentic love for their children is always aligned with the truth. In the case of gender dysphoria, this means recognising that happiness and peace will not be found in rejecting the truth of the human person and the human body. Thus parents must resist simplistic solutions presented by advocates of Gender Ideology and strive to discover and address the real reasons for their children's pain and unhappiness. They should seek out trustworthy clinicians for sound counsel. Meeting with other parents who have been through similar trials also can be a source of strength and support.

The child needs to be informed over and over again about the love of God for them. A useful narrative for their child is possibly something like this:

"Every one of us has a struggle that is unique. Your struggle is that you feel alienated from your body, as though you are supposed to have a different one. Your parents believe you when you tell us about the pain and anguish, and we shall always be by your side. But, please know that, although you may struggle with your body or self-image, God's unrelenting love for you means that He loves all of you, which includes your body. Our obligation to respect and care for the body comes from the fact that your body is part of the person God made whom God loves with an infinite love. Be on guard against simplistic solutions that promise relief from your struggles by the change of name, pronouns or even the appearance of your body. There are many who have walked that path before you only to regret it. The difficult but more promising path to joy and peace is to work with a trusted counsellor, therapist, priest and/or friend to come to an awareness of the goodness of your body and of your identity as male or female.

"Listen to the Catholic Church; she possesses the wisdom of God. The Church desires to bring you the love of Jesus Christ himself. The Church is here to assist and accompany you on this journey, so that you will know the beauty of the body and soul that God gave you and experience true peace in your heart."

Chapter 13

The Law and Gender Ideology

Advocates of Gender Ideology see the law as an important means to both spread belief in the ideology and to assuage the pain persons who suffer gender dysphoria undergo. The campaign goes as far as to request that the person themselves can decide, independent of any external adjudicator, their gender. For example, the powerful and highly influential doctors' union, the British Medical Association, has published support for this type of proposal on the grounds of individual choice (autonomy) being the number-one guide to truth. (94)

On a very simple level, this seems far removed from any objective test of common sense. This type of freedom has the capacity to let a male prisoner move into a female prison for an easier sentence. It allows a boy to decide he likes to change into his football kit in the girls' changing room or enables a girl to deceive a boy on a date that he believes is a person who really is a potential marriage partner.

The law conveys powerful messages. Many believe the maxim if the law says x is true, then x is true.

While clearly the law should defend all persons from ridicule, abuse and violence, the calls go much deeper. The call is for the law to state that what a person says is what is reality. This is an unjust law since it not only helps affirm the individual person who suffers gender non-conformity into objective unrealityi also serves to offer others an intellectual framework for behaviours that damage themselves and others.

Also, escalating reporting rates in the young of gender fluidity are suggestive of the phenomenon of contagion, making others believe they have the problem when they do not. Certainly, contagion occurs in many psychiatric conditions when groups of young people associate in close proximity.

As with professionals in the spheres of medicine, nursing, social work and law, those in education are now potentially at risk from laws that give priority to individual autonomy over the conscientious objection of employees regarding pronoun reversal. This is a new territory for teachers. It means that there can now be, in their place of work, an issue requiring conscientious objection on the grounds of their faith and praxis.

In terms of Catholic school there is a potential nonsense evolving in the law where the school is free to teach orthodoxy but is not free to reinforce this by orthopraxis even though the school was clearly founded on teaching and practising within its walls the ten commandments. On both sides of the debate informed protagonists agree that opinions of the pupils are formed by the actions of their teachers speaking louder than words. Therefore, it is not surprising that there is a developing battle.

For these reasons, and many others, it is not just to make the law an instrument to promulgate errors.

Conclusion

This book started with the words of Pope Francis:
"Gender Ideology is demonic!"

Is this mere metaphorical medieval exaggeration or a serious warning about a real grave danger to humanity?

There is no doubt the Pope meant it literally!

Gender Justice is a response to this grave danger. This battle involves malign supernatural forces that no human mind can fully comprehend that have the capacity to cause immense harm to millions of people. This little book is offered as one weapon in the armamentarium.

Gender Ideology is a deep rebellion against God.

Not accepting that human beings are created as man or woman goes against experience, against nature, against reason and against science. It is a lie that originates from the father of lies, the Devil. An ideology that can capture the common sense of people and become a dominant ideology of our time needs much more than human power to command such a degree of respect.

Behaviours change when principles change. If the principle that human life has a relative rather than absolute worth is adopted, then abortion occurs. If the principle that private property is a communal possession not a personal possession, then non-consensual expropriation occurs. And if the principle of inherent racial inferiority is adopted, then apartheid gets a matrix to practise racial segregation. Gender Ideology is a new principle with massive potential to change behaviours for the worse.

The smell of powers beyond the natural order is apparent. Just ask how is it that the touchstone of being judged as somebody who respects or does not respect human rights is the adoption of a rainbow flag? A casual day-to day glance at the media confirms the pervasive inculcation of this opinion.

In a world where girls are often denied education, millions go hungry every day, unborn children are killed with reckless abandon and countless women are the victims of violence and abuse, still these issues do not command the human rights cause célèbre spot. Instead, an issue that all agree in quantitative terms is a minority one takes front stage. This is bizarre. It would be like denying that the Holocaust was the number-one human rights issue in Nazi Germany and replacing it as the touchstone of anti-Nazism with a more remote, minority problem such as the Nazi obsession with replacing non-German art with German alternatives. Most Germans and indeed English people, then and now, do not really care who creates the paintings or sculpts the statues!

It is the effect on marriage and family that is the prime practical danger of Gender Ideology in terms of calculable effects.

The concept of the existence of two innate genders that are designed with an inherent compatibility to unite physically, psychologically and spiritually is destroyed by adopting ideas that gender is a man-made construct. Without a binary view of equal, different, but uniquely compatible genders, then marriage as an innate calling designed as a lifelong union of a man and a woman becomes a nonsense. Rendering marriage a nonsense then leaves the best way to nurture children a matter of opinion. Childcare is then judged equivalent if it is arbitrarily deemed to meet certain material standards. A loving mum and dad are not necessarily the best a child can get. Accepting Gender Ideology means marriage has no particular advantage to children, and by logical progression, since children are the building blocks of society, marriage has no predominant role as the optimum way to develop a healthy society. In the final analysis, the gender battle is a battle to give children what is best.

Gender Ideology is a potent new intellectual framework forming a principle to provoke and encourage the development of marital destruction, causing great harm to the vulnerable in the process. If gender has no meaning to dictate the purpose of a fulfilled human existence, then as a logical accompaniment of this, marriage is of no consequence to the wellbeing of the human person. But this is social science gibberish.

Population studies time and time again show the outcomes for married couples and their children are best in whatever parameter one chooses, be it mortality, morbidity, economic wellbeing, life chances, educational achievement, criminality … The list is endless. (95)

Obviously, there is an economic argument to contest this view. It is impossible to conduct a scientific study that proves it one way or the other. Married couples are often richer so outcomes are better, so it is said let us just make everybody as rich and the difference in outcomes will be annulled. But if the marriage state solves the precipitating problem in the first place (i.e. a protector of economic security), then why not just use the proven means? It makes sense. Why reinvent the wheel?

It may be true to say that all non-marital intimate relationships, be they cohabitation, polyamorous partnerships, divorce and re-marriage arrangements, "throuples," same-sex partnerships or even peripatetic siring fathers, share to some degree elements of commitment and permanency ranging from negligible to significant. But only a publicly ratified solemn promise of a man for a woman or a woman for a man saying, "I am here for you and our children, forever, come what may", what we call marriage, has the divine guarantee and inscription in the core of our being that this is what human beings are made for.

Gender ideologists are keen to express their views as simply being an individual relatively benign political view so as everybody can live in a more equitable manner harming nobody.(96) It is said with sincerity and it is possible to see in the writings the possibility that they have personally experienced painful situations that have formed their (false) conclusions.

But actually this is not just a relatively benign political choice like voting for the Labour or Conservative party. It is a profound battle about what is reality? (97) It has implications for everybody in the depths of their being. This is why this book is titled gender justice because human beings thrive when they follow the real truth about their nature and are harmed when they do not. This is clear from reason. If a person believes that reality dictates that they can fly they certainly can experience the joy of flying when they jump off a cliff. They can even take others along with them. Many may be convinced. But they cannot escape the rocks at the bottom of the cliff when their free fall finishes, real truth kicks in.

No man is an island, the actions of one man effect the actions of others so it is a false proposition to contend that the individual's invention of truth contrary to reality cannot have both a destructive and indoctrinating effect on the whole of society.

The harm gender ideology does to those unfortunate individuals who suffer Gender Non-Conformity is the tip of the iceberg. Nobody of course wakes up in the morning hoping to have a gender identity issue, nobody chooses this in the sense of desiring to bring pain and confusion into their life. But to offer a false concept of reality to these suffering brothers and sisters of ours as the solution is adding insult to injury. The harm of the ideology however goes far beyond the individual patient. As Pope Francis said:

, "Gender Ideology is a war against marriage and the family." (98) It is a war that Christians are called to fight as a responsibility of love towards our neighbour.

.

References

1. Cardinal Versaldi, G et al. (2019) Male and Female He Created Them. Towards a path of dialogue on the question of Gender Theory in Education. Vatican Press. London, UK: CTS Publications. Released for publication with the permission of Pope Francis.

2. Dilsaver, G. (2017) Celebrating God Given Gender. 1st Edition. New York: Imago Dei Press.

3. The CTS New Catholic Bible. (2008) 1st Edition. Book of Genesis 5:1–2. London: Harper Collins Publications.

4. Magnuson, E et al. (2012) 1st Edition. Gender and Culture in Psychology, Theories and Practices. Cambridge, UK: Cambridge University Press.

5. Morgenroth, T et al. (2018) Gender Trouble in Social Psychology: How Can Butler's Work Inform Experimental Social Psychologists' Conceptualization of Gender? Frontiers in Psychology, 27 Jul 2018, 9:1320.

6. Holmes, M. (2007) 1st Edition. What is Gender? London: Sage Publications.

7. Butler, J. (1990) 1st Edition. Gender Trouble. Abingdon-on-Thames, UK: Routledge.

8. Australia National University. Gender Inclusive Handbook. Accessed online on 29/04/21 at 1700 hours at: https://genderinstitute.anu.edu.au/.../Gender_inclusive_handbook.pdf

9. Owen, G. Nine-Year-Old Children and Gender. Mail online 23/01/21. Accessed on 02/05/21 at: https://www.dailymail.co.uk/news/article-9179703.

10. de Beauvoir, S. (1949) 1st Edition. The Second Sex. London: Penguin.

11. Butler, J. (2006) 1st Edition. Gender Trouble: Feminism and the Subversion of Identity. Abingdon, UK: Routledge Publications.

12. Butler, J. (2004) 1st Edition. Undoing Gender. Abingdon, UK: Routledge Publications.

13. Fausto-Sterling, A. (2000) 1st Edition. Sexing the Body: Gender Politics and the Construction of Sexuality. New York: Basic Books Publications.

14. Blackless, M et al. (2000) How sexually dimorphic are we? American Journal of Human Biology. 11 February 2000. 12: 151–166.

15. Cardinal Versaldi, G et al. (2019) Male and Female He Created Them. Towards a path of dialogue on the question of Gender Theory in Education. London, UK: CTS Publications. Released for publication with the permission of Pope Francis.

16. Ambras Syndrome (Werewolf Syndrome.) Accessed online on 14/06/21 at: https://syndromespedia.com/ambras-syndrome.html.

17. Bermejo-Sánchez, E et al. Phocomelia: a worldwide descriptive epidemiologic study in a large series of cases from the International Clearinghouse for Birth Defects Surveillance and Research, and overview of the literature. American Journal of Medical Genetics. November 2011. 157C (4): 305–320.

18. Lund, P. Oculocutaneous albinism in Southern Africa: population structure, health, and genetic care. Annals of Human Biology. 2005. Mar–Apr 32(2): 168–73.

19. Darwin, C. (2013) first published 1871. Reprinted. Descent of Man. Ware, UK: Wordsworth.

20. Lu, C. et al. Identifying and Interpreting Apparent Neanderthal Ancestry in African Individuals. Published in

Cell. 20 February 2020.

21. Teen with male genitalia raised as a boy pregnant after discovering ovaries. Accessed online on 16 June 2021 at:www.mirror.co.uk/news/us-news/teen-male-genitalia-raised-boy

22. Wisniewski, A. et al. Congenital micropenis: long-term medical, surgical, and psychosexual follow-up of individuals raised male or female. Hormone Research. 2001. 56(1–2): 3–11.

23. Williams, W et al. (2019) First printed 1992. Two Spirits. Texas, USA: Peregrine Ventures.

24. McClure, L. (2002) 1st Edition. Sexuality and gender in the classical world: Interpreting ancient history. Oxford, UK: Blackwell.

25. Lupa. (2007) 1st Edition. A Field Guide to Otherkin. Stafford, UK: Megalithica Books.

26. Niyaz, N. (2017) 1st Edition. Metaphorical Framing, the Sapir-Whorf-Hypothesis and how language shapes our thoughts. Germany: Grin Verlag.

27. Dixon, H et al. Stonewall urges employers to drop mother for 'parent who has given birth' to boost equality ranking. 3 June 2021. London: The Telegraph newspaper.

28. The CTS New Catholic Bible. (2008) 1st Edition. Gospel of St Mark 12:30. London: Harper Collins Publications.

29. The CTS New Catholic Bible. (2008) 1st Edition. Book of Genesis 5: 1–2. London: Harper Collins Publications.

30. The CTS New Catholic Bible. (2008) 1st Edition. Book of Genesis 1:31. London: Harper Collins Publications.

31. Transgender and pronouns. Bishop of Arlington Diocese USA. Accessed online on 01/07/21 at: www.catholicculture.org/culture/library/view.cfmrecnm =12554

32. Stein, E. (1996) 2nd Edition. Essays on Women. Washington, USA: ICS Publications.

33. St Pope John Paul II. (1995) Letter to Women. London: CTS Publications.

34. Petter, O. How can men support women against misogyny and violence? 11 March 2021. London: The Independent newspaper.

35. Edwards, C. (1993) 1st Edition. The Politics of Immorality in Ancient Rome. Cambridge, UK: Cambridge University Press.

36. Aquinas, T. (2008) Reprinted from original. Summa Theologiae, The Gospel of Grace. Volume 30: 1a2ae. 106–114. Cambridge, UK: Cambridge University Press.

37. St John Paul II. (1988) On the Blessed Virgin Mary in the life of the Pilgrim Church. London, UK: CTS Publications.

38. The CTS New Catholic Bible. (2008) 1st Edition. Book of Ecclesiasticus 1:2. London: Harper Collins Publications.

39. St Pope John Paul II. (2006) 1st Edition. Man and Woman, He Created Them. London: Pauline Books and Media.

40. Schwartz, C. (2013) 2nd Edition. X Chromosome. Brenner's Encyclopaedia of Genetics. Salt Lake City, USA: Academic Press.

41. Shah, K et al. Do you know the sex of your cells? American Journal of Physiology. Published 6 November 2013.

42. Patrone, D. (2009) Disfigured anatomies and imperfect analogies: body integrity identity disorder and the supposed right to self-demanded amputation of healthy body parts. Journal of Medical Ethics. 2009. 35(9).

43. Aquinas, T. Summa Theologica, Pt. 1, Q. 75, art. 3. Accessed online on 16/06/21 at: www.documenta-catholica. eu/d_1225-1274- Thomas Aquinas - Summa Theologiae - Prima Pars - EN.pdf

44. Feser, E. (2019) 1st Edition. Aristotle's Revenge: The Metaphysical Foundations of Physical and Biological Science. Smitten Germany: Editiones Scholasticae.
45. Descartes, Rene. Translated from original 1999. First published 1664. Discourse on Method and the Meditations. London: Penguin Classics.

46. St Pope John Paul II. (1994) 1st Edition. Crossing the Threshold of Hope. New York, USA: Knopf.

47. Furudi, A. (2016) 1st Edition. The Moral Case for Abortion. London: Palgrave Macmillan.

48. McDonald-Gibson, C. Child Euthanasia in Belgium. 13 February 2016. London: The Independent newspaper.

49. France-Presse, A. Dutch Court Approves Euthanasia in Advanced Case of Dementia. 21 April 2020. London: The Guardian newspaper.

50. Sullivan, Scott. Why Transgenderism is Wrong: A Critique of the Philosophical Assumptions Behind Modern Transgender Theory. Accessed online on 21/06/21 at: www.

catholic.com/magazine/online-edition/one-way-to-debunk-transgender-philosophy.

51. Aristotle. (2018) 1st Edition. On the Soul. Oxford, UK: OUP.

52. Diagnostic Statistical and Manual of Mental Disorders. (2013) Fifth Edition. American Psychiatric Association Publications.

53. ibid

54. Saul, H. Pope Francis compares arguments for transgender rights to nuclear arms race. 21 February 2015. London: The Independent newspaper.

55. Osbourne, S. Pope Francis says gender theory is part of a 'global war' on marriage and family. 2 October 2016. London: The Independent newspaper.

56. Pope Francis. Pontiff laments children being taught gender is choice—Pontiff says predecessor labels current times an epoch of sin against God the Creator.
2 August 2016. Dublin: Irish Independent newspaper.

57. Pope Francis. (2016) Amoris Laetitia. London: Catholic Truth Society.

58. Nelson Tebbe, Deborah Widiss and Shannon Gilreath, Debate, The Argument for Same-Sex Marriage. Accessed online on 20/05/21 at: www.pennumbra.com/debates/ pdfs/ Marriage.pdf.

59. Holland, T. (2019) 1st Edition. Dominion. London: Little Brown Publishers.

60. Twitter, @jk_rowling, 6 June 2020. <https://twitter.com/

jk_rowling/status/1269389298664701952>.

61. Haug, W et al. (2000) 1ˢᵗ Edition. The Demographic Characteristics of the Linguistic and Religious Groups in Switzerland—The Demographic Characteristics of National Minorities in Certain European States Strasbourg: Council of Europe Directorate General III, Social Cohesion Publications.

62. Hughes, D et al. 2012. 1st Edition. Brain-Based Parenting. New York: Norton and Company.

63. Cardinal Versaldi, G et al. (2019) Male and Female He Created Them. Towards a path of dialogue on the question of Gender Theory in Education. Vatican Press. London, UK: CTS Publications. Released for publication with the permission of Pope Francis.

64. Furtado, P et al. Gender dysphoria associated with disorders of sex development. National Review of Urology. 2012. 9(11): 620–627.

65. Zhou, Jiang-Ning et al. A Sex Difference in the Human Brain and its Relation to Transsexuality. Nature. 02/11/95. 37: 68–70.

66. Strain, L et al. A True Hermaphrodite Chimera Resulting from Embryo Amalgamation after in Vitro Fertilization. New England Journal of Medicine. 15 January 1998. 338: 166–169.

67. Kolb, B et al. (2016) 1ˢᵗ Edition. An introduction to brain and Behaviour. New York, USA: Worth.

68. Heylens, G et al. Gender identity disorder in twins: a review of the case report literature. The Journal of Sexual Medicine. 3 March 2012. 9(3): 751–7.

69. Joost à Campo et al. Psychiatric Comorbidity of Gender Identity Disorders: A Survey Among Dutch Psychiatrists. 1 July 2003. American Journal of Psychiatry.

70. Sexual differentiation of the human brain: relation to gender identity, sexual orientation and neuropsychiatric disorders, US National Library of Medicine National Institutes of Health, Frontiers in Neuroendocrinology, April 2011.

71. Pazzagli, A et al. Dysphoria and aloneness in borderline personality disorder. Psychopathology. Jul–Aug 2000. 33(4): 220–6.

72. Colizzo, M et al. Dissociative symptoms in individuals with gender dysphoria: Is the elevated prevalence real? Psychiatry Research. 30 March 2015. 226(1): 173–180.

73. Marchiano, L. et al. Outbreak: On Transgender Teens and Psychic Epidemics. Psychological Perspectives. A Quarterly Journal of Jungian Thought. 6 October 2017. 60(3): Gender Diversity.

74. Press Association. Boy 'living life entirely as a girl' removed from mother's care by judge. 21 October 2016. London: The Guardian newspaper. 75. Hines, S. (2018) 1st Edition. Is Gender Fluid? London, UK: Thames and Hudson.

76. Cowan, W et al. The Human Genome Project and its Impact on Psychiatry, Annual Review of Neuroscience. 2002. 25: 1–50

77. Feilden, T. Most scientists 'can't replicate studies by their peers'. Science correspondent, BBC Today programme 22/02/17. Accessed online 16/05/21 at: www.bbc.co.uk/news/science-environment-39054778

78. The CTS New Catholic Bible. (2008) 1st Edition. Genesis 1:28. London: Harper Collins Publications.

79. The CTS New Catholic Bible. (2008) 1st Edition. Gospel of Mathew 10:28. London: Harper Collins Publications.80. The CTS New Catholic Bible. (2008) 1st Edition. Genesis 5:2. London: Harper Collins Publications.

81. Baker, S. Transgender teenager who was born with male genitalia and raised as a boy is now four months pregnant after discovering she has functioning female reproductive organs. 16 November 2020. Published in Mail online. Accessed online on 13/05/21 at: www.dailymail.co.uk/femail/article-8953527/Teenager-raised-boy-four-months-pregnant.html

82. H. Kitano. Systems Biology: A Brief Overview. Science 295.5560 (March 1, 2002): 1662–1664.

83. Dixon, H. 3rd June 2021. Stonewall urges employers to drop mother for 'parent who has given birth' to boost equality ranking. London: The Telegraph newspaper.

84. St Pope John Paul II. Fides et Ratio. (1998) 1st Edition. London: Catholic Truth Society.

85. St Pope John Paul II. The Acting Person. (1979) 1st Edition in English. London: Springer Publications.

86. Haas, A et al. (2014) Suicide Attempts among Gender Non-Conforming Adults. Accessed online on 23/05/21 at: https://williamsinstitute.law.ucla.edu/research/suicide-attemptsamong-transgender-and-gender-non-conforming-adults

87. Pike, M. Dad of Trans son Stormy, 4 years old, Testimony. Daily Mirror online. Accessed online on 2/4/21 at: www.mirror.co.uk/tv/tv-news/father-trans-son-4-says-24076135

88. Pope Francis. (2016) Amoris Laetitia. London: Catholic Truth Society.

89. National Health Service Gender Non-Conformity. Accessed online on 2/4/21 at: www.nhs.uk/conditions/gender-dysphoria/treatment

90. Costa, R. et al. The effect of cross-sex hormonal treatment on gender dysphoria individuals' mental health: a systematic

review. Neuropsychiatry Disease and Treatment. 4 Aug 2016; 12:1953–66.

91. Nota, N et al. Occurrence of Acute Cardiovascular Events in Transgender Individuals Receiving Hormone Therapy-Results From a Large Cohort Study. Circulation. 2019; 139:1461–1462.

92. Dhejne, C et al. Long-term follow-up of transsexual persons undergoing sex reassignment surgery: cohort study in Sweden 201. Published online by free to access www.plosone.org 1st February 2011, Volume 6, Issue 2. Accessed on 3/05/21 at: www.journals.plos.org/plosone/article?id=10.1371/journal.pone.0016885

93. Catechism of the Catholic Church. (1994) 1st Edition. London: Geoffrey Chapman.

94. Trueland, J. 16/09/20. Push for progress on transgender rights in healthcare. British Medical Association Journal. Accessed online on 23/03/21 at: www.bma.org.uk/news-and-opinion/push-for-progress-on-transgender-rights-in-healthcare

95. Wilcox, B et al. (2011) 3rd Edition. Why Marriage Matters. Thirty Conclusions from Social Scientists. New York: Broadway Publications.

96. Buttler, J The Backlash against "Gender Ideology" must stop. London: The New Statesman 21st January 2019

97 ibid

98. Osbourne, S. Pope Francis says gender theory is part of a 'global war' on marriage and family. 02/10/16. London: The Independent newspaper.